Triangulating Archaeological Landscapes:
The US Coast Survey in California, 1850–1895

R. Scott Byram

Number 65
Contributions of the Archaeological Research Facility
University of California, Berkeley

© 2013 Regents of the University of California

Published by eScholarship, Berkeley, CA ISBN:

978-0-9890022-1-9

1st Edition

Available open access at:

http://escholarship.org/uc/item/6tt003pf

Cover image: portion of T-sheet no. 1497A, Salt Point to Fisherman's Bay, 1878

Contents

Preface and Acknowledgments vi

Chapter 1 Nineteenth-Century Science on the Pacific Coast 1
    Agency History 9
    USCS Archaeological Research 13

**Chapter 2 Situated Cultural Description:
California T-sheets and Field Notebooks** 15
    Triangulation and Topographic Mapping 16
    Research with the USCS Collection at NARA II 18

**Chapter 3 Maps, Notes, and Sketches in Archaeological
Interpretation: Colonial Sites** 25
    Cities and Towns 25
    Landings 27
    Early Industrial Sites 32
    Shipwrecks and Related Sites 34
    Fortifications 39
    Ranchos and Adobes 41

**Chapter 4 Maps, Notes, and Sketches in Archaeological
Interpretation: Native American Sites** 49
    Native American Villages 49
    Archaeological Mound Sites 54

**Chapter 5 The Rediscovery of Camp Castaway
and the Wreck of the *Captain Lincoln*** 66
    US Coast Survey Maps 67
    Site Survey: 2010–2011 69

Chapter 6 Discussion and Conclusions 76
    The Structure of USCS Research in Archaeology 76
    New Research Directions 79
    The Urgency of USCS Archival Analysis 80
    Triangulating Site Histories 82

Appendix 83

References 98

List of Illustrations

Figures

Figure 1 Theodolite 1
Figure 2 Triangulation using a theodolite 1
Figure 3 Topographic mapping with a plane table and alidade 2
Figure 4 US Coast Survey reconnaissance party 2
Figure 5 Portion of T-sheet no. 1396, Santa Rosa Island 3
Figure 6 Plane table mapping, Sacramento Delta 4
Figure 7 Port Rumiantsev on T-sheet no. 883 5
Figure 8 Drawing of Presidio Hill Station 6
Figure 9 Map of Presidio Hill Station and vicinity 6
Figure 10 Map of Ellis Landing area 7
Figure 11 Page from Forney's notebook 8
Figure 12 Shell Mound Station 9
Figure 13 The US Coast Survey brig *Fauntleroy* 10
Figure 14 US Coast and Geodetic Survey ship *Active* 11
Figure 15 US Coast Survey party at San Luis Obispo 11
Figure 16 1851–1852 map of Sausalito Station 19
Figure 17 Mound Station near Loon Point 20
Figure 18 Ruins of the Cedro (Ysidro) Reyes adobe 21
Figure 19 Santa Monica Station and setting 22
Figure 20 Page from USCGS T-sheet index 23
Figure 21 Portion of T-sheet no. 360 showing Oakland in 1852 24
Figure 22 The UC Berkeley campus in 1873 26
Figure 23 Fort Ross area, 1878 28

Figure 24	Map of Seal Bluff Landing	29
Figure 25	Drawing of Seal Bluff Landing	29
Figure 26	Chinese fishing community, Point Molate	30
Figure 27	Anaheim Landing Station	31
Figure 28	Santa Cruz primary triangulation station	33
Figure 29	Pacific Salt Works	35
Figure 30	Map of Magdalena Bay, Baja California, Mexico	36
Figure 31	Presidio Wharf House Station	38
Figure 32	USS *Edith* wreck	39
Figure 33	Fort Mervine and El Castillo in Monterey	41
Figure 34	Old Adobe and Old Town stations	42
Figure 35	Lowry Ranch, 1876	44
Figure 36	Preliminary sketch of Santa Barbara	52
Figure 37	1851 sketch of Mission San Luis Rey	54
Figure 38	Map of San Nicolas Island and the lone woman's cave	55
Figure 39	Description of the lone woman's cave	56
Figure 40	Shell mound near Candlestick Point	59
Figure 41	Description and map of Guano Island	62
Figure 42	1861 description of Wreck Station	68
Figure 43	Ground-penetrating radar at Camp Castaway	70
Figure 44	Camp Castaway excavation, 2012	70
Figure 45	Excavation at Camp Castaway	71
Figure 46	Structural artifacts recovered at Camp Castaway	73
Figure 47	Pre–Civil War ammunition recovered at Camp Castaway	74
Figure 48	Domestic artifacts recovered at Camp Castaway	75

Tables

Table 1   Archaeologically recorded colonial sites updated with USCS records 46
Table 2   Colonial sites recognized by USCS surveyors as archaeological or in ruins 47
Table 3   Colonial sites documented by the USCS with no confirmed archaeological remains .. 48
Table 4   Archaeologically recorded Native American sites updated with USCS records 64
Table 5   Native American archaeological sites identified by the USCS 64
Table 6   Other precontact and mission-era sites or possible sites 65

Preface and Acknowledgments

I began researching the USCS collections at the National Archives while a graduate student in the Department of Anthropology at the University of Oregon. I conducted research during annual visits to my father's home in the Washington, DC, area, so the research progressed slowly but steadily. I had learned the value of archival research for archaeology and ethnography as a participant in collaborative Native American ethnographic and historical research between the University of Oregon and the Coquille Indian Tribe. Jon Erlandson, Madonna Moss, Don Ivy, George Wasson, Mark Tveskov, David Lewis, and many others contributed much time and energy to the groundbreaking Southwest Oregon Research Project. Concurrently, as I sought new avenues for my research on Native American weir fishing archaeological sites on the Oregon coast, I encountered the maps and field notes of the USCS and realized these records were of remarkable value to the archaeologists and historians of the Pacific coast. However the collection was not readily accessible (and became even less so as large manuscript maps were removed from direct access by researchers in the past decade). After my initial reports on the collection, there were a few subsequent studies in Oregon, but much of the USCS collection remained unexamined by archaeologists for several years.

When I became a visiting scholar at the UC Berkeley Archaeological Research Facility (ARF) in 2007, a major focus was assessing the scope and relevance of this collection for Pacific coast archaeology, with an emphasis on California and Oregon. Professors Kent Lightfoot and Margaret Conkey of UC Berkeley have been inspiring mentors. Collaborations with Dr. Lightfoot, Tsim Schneider, and Nico Tripcevich have opened new directions for applications of US Coast Survey records in archaeology and tribal cultural heritage studies. Other UC Berkeley professors who contributed to the completion of this volume in the Contributions series include Christine Hastorf, Laurie Wilkie, Ruth Tringham, Beth Piatote, Jun Sunseri, and Junko Habu. While conducting research in DC, I was very fortunate to meet Dr. John Cloud and Captain Albert "Skip" Theberge of NOAA Central Library, two historians who have long seen the value of the US Coast Survey maps at the National Archives. I continue to benefit from their histories of the agency and explanation of nineteenth-century surveying methods. Dr. Cloud provided me with numerous scans of T-sheets in what are still somewhat cumbersome file sizes, and small portions of several of these appear in this monograph.

The geographic scope of the research presented here includes some areas where I had little or no experience before this project. As such I relied on local and topical expertise for some of the sites discussed. Individuals who assisted in California include archaeologists Steve Schwartz, Jon Erlandson, René Vellanoweth, Marla Mealey, Jim Allan, Leigh Jordan, and Bob Schwemmer, and historians Linda Bentz and Ann Huston. Archaeologists who have collaborated with me on Oregon USCS-related projects include Mark Tveskov, Jim Thomson, Jim Delgado, Dennis Griffin, Darby Shindruk, Sarah Purdy-Silbernagel, Susan White, Mike Knight, Reg Pullen, and Steve Samuels. Tribal heritage specialists who contributed to this study include Don Ivy, Robert Kentta, Nicole Norris, Agnes Castronuevo, and Tsim Schneider. Archaeologist Darby Shindruk, design editor Carl Andrews, and copyeditor Lee Steadman helped me to prepare the volume. I am also grateful for the valuable input provided by the three anonymous reviewers. My children Twyla and Diego provide creative inspiration for my work.

Chapter 1
Nineteenth–Century Science on the Pacific Coast

On January 10, 1849, the schooner *Ewing* sailed from New York Harbor bound for California. Unlike many other ships on this route carrying miners, merchants, and speculators during the Gold Rush, this was a US government vessel. The schooner transported a team of surveyors whose mission was to chart the waters of the eastern Pacific for maritime commerce and national defense. They were members of the US Coast Survey (USCS), whose maps and charts were known by navigators throughout the world for their accuracy and detail (Barnard 1858; Gudde 1951). When the *Ewing* arrived at San Francisco on August 1st, the surveyors disembarked with crates holding alidades, plane tables, theodolites, and spirit levels—the field equipment needed to produce maps and charts, field notes, drawings, and other scientific records (Figures 1–3). Though delayed until the following year because of the difficulties of maintaining a ship's crew during the height of the Gold Rush (Theberge 2006), by the spring of 1850 the Pacific coast surveyors had set up offices in San Francisco and mapping was well underway (Cloud 2007).

Over the next 50 years the US Coast Survey generated a vast quantity of manuscript records depicting the history of Pacific seaboard settlement, urban and industrial

Figure 1 Theodolite typical of those used by the US Coast Survey in the 1860s. (Courtesy of NOAA Central Library.)

Figure 2 Triangulation using a theodolite, US Coast and Geodetic Survey. (Courtesy of NOAA Central Library.)

development, and transportation infrastructure. The scientists who conducted these surveys traveled by horseback (Figure 4), wagon, and ship, linking many details of the routes to survey positions. They often depicted significant archaeological and historical sites among other contextual information in their maps, notes, and sketches (Figure 5). In their efforts to plot nearby landmarks as references for future surveyors to find the survey markers again, they mapped and described shell mounds, caves and trails, embarcaderos and harbors, and innumerable structures ranging from bark lodges, earthworks, and adobe ruins to nascent city blocks.

Although increasingly used for ecological research in this region, the US Coast Survey records have yet to find their place as baseline data for archaeological research in California. In many cases, map coordinates and descriptions of former shell mounds, adobe ruins, and other types of sites have been published from these records that have yet to be incorporated into regional archaeological studies. Additionally, there are hundreds of unpublished nineteenth-century maps, field notebook pages, and sketches in the USCS archives that depict many significant archaeological sites.

The records cover the entire shoreline and tidewater reaches of the state, as well as the shorelines of Baja California and the Northwest Coast. Some inland areas were also mapped (Figure 6).

Figure 3 Topographic mapping with a plane table and alidade on the Pacific coast, US Coast and Geodetic Survey. These maps and field notebooks are now at the National Archives and Records Administration II (NARA II) in College Park, Maryland. (Courtesy of NOAA Central Library.)

Figure 4 US Coast Survey reconnaissance party on the California coast. (Courtesy of NOAA Central Library.)

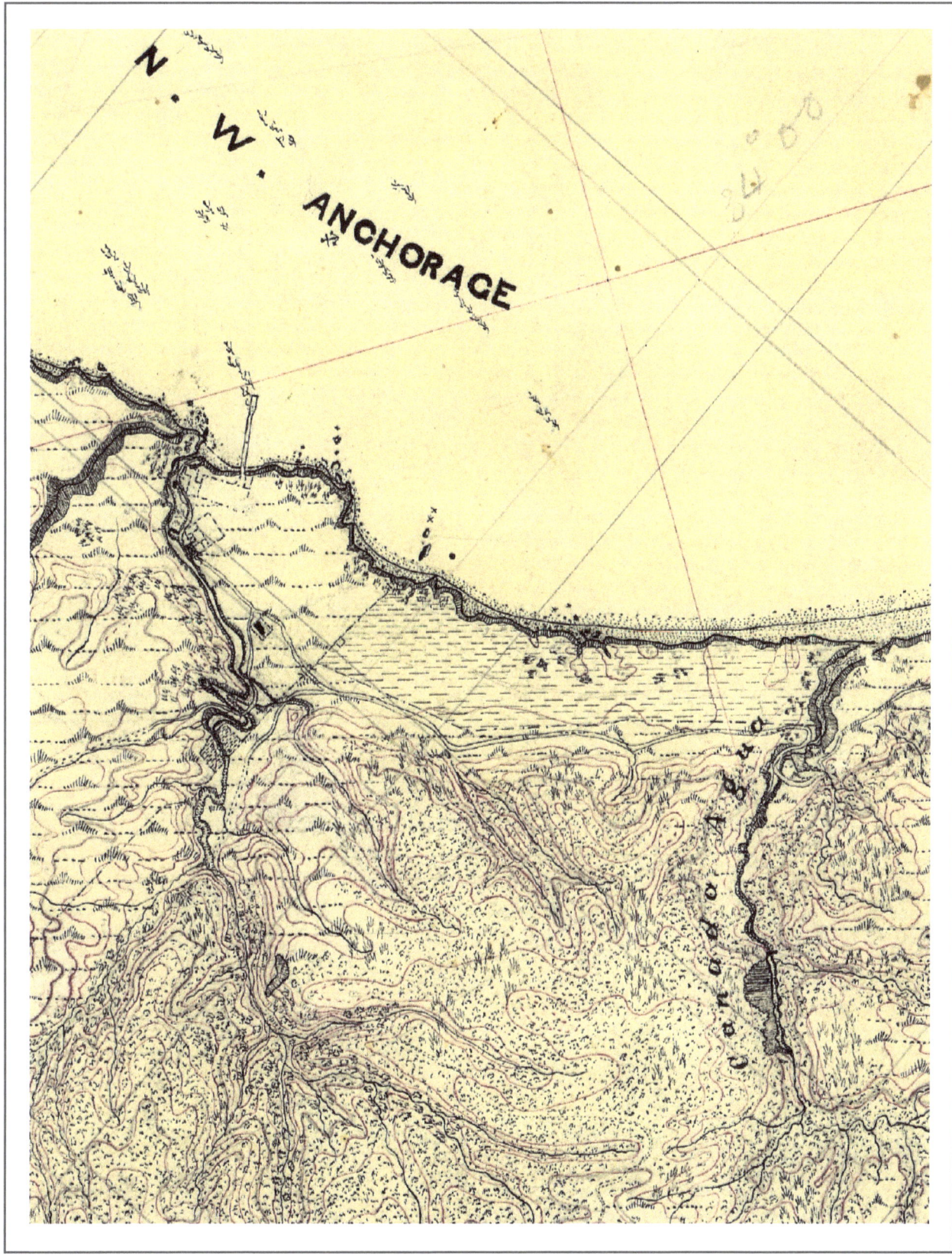

Figure 5 Portion of T-sheet no. 1396, Santa Rosa Island (Forney 1872). Red lines are topographic contours; also depicted are kelp beds, grasslands, plowed acreage, chaparral, beach, roads, buildings, fences, and a wharf. (Scanned by John Cloud at NARA II.)

Figure 6 Plane table mapping, Sacramento Delta. (Courtesy of NOAA Central Library.)

This volume presents examples of the more distinctive records in the USCS collection, but it only scratches the surface in terms of the collection's scope and relevance for California archaeology.

That much of this material arrives rather late to California archaeology is surprising in light of the role some of the surveyors played in the development of the University of California and the California Academy of Sciences. While university researchers were the first to do archaeology in the context of anthropology, they were not the first scientists to accurately map and describe many West Coast archaeological sites and other sites of historical significance. The USCS surveyors preceded archaeologists by decades at several sites, documenting topography, historical associations, and period context. Addressing these records in light of later archaeological and historical studies can greatly enhance interpretations of site structure and other variability.

Specifically, USCS maps and location descriptions allow the archaeologist to confirm and characterize previously identified sites and features, to locate sites and features that are reported but not yet confirmed, and to identify new sites or site components. They provide additional data for interpretations of sites based on other archival sources, oral history, and archaeological data. These records expand our understanding of site context with detailed topography, vegetation cover, and infrastructure details at set points in time. And because surveyors were primarily interested in describing settings for later relocation of survey markers, their descriptions often portray details that may not be evident in many other types of records, such as the use of a particular building or the ethnicity of people living at or near a mapped location. Unlike many graphic portrayals of the era, USCS maps and sketches are rarely embellished, having a strong emphasis on structures and other physical infrastructure such as roads, fences, and water sources. These characteristics mean that USCS records are well suited to incorporation in archaeological analysis at a variety of scales.

Much of the USCS collection remains relatively inaccessible, but growing digital access will eventually open this resource for widespread use. Previous use of these records has largely been limited to lower-resolution published maps, charts, reports, and microfilmed records at the National Archives and Records Administration II (NARA) in College Park, Maryland, and to a lesser degree to the small number of hand-drawn topographic maps that have been scanned or photocopied.

This study presents 33 images of maps, sketches, and field notes from nineteenth-century surveys, most previously unpublished. It discusses over 50 archaeological sites that were documented to some extent by the US Coast Survey in the nineteenth century, emphasizing that the agency's maps and reports are most valuable when examined along with the field notes and geographic data recorded by the surveyors.

USCS scientific records include some of the earliest archaeological and historical site mapping in California using precision survey instruments. Several well-known sites were mapped, described, or sketched during the early 1850s, before the expanse of US settlement had reconfigured many shoreline landscapes. In many cases the USCS permanently monumented locations and later published their geographic coordinates. Sites and features were recorded as reference information for relocating the survey station marker that was being mapped. For example, the Russian buildings of Port Rumiantsev were among the few structures on Bodega Head peninsula, and therefore they were mapped with precision relative to Bodega Head Station (Figure 7). The Presidio of San Francisco was sketched and mapped as a reference for nearby Presidio Hill Station (Figures 8 and 9). And numerous shell mounds on coastal plains were depicted because they were distinctive and comparatively permanent landmarks relative to other features of the surrounding plain (Figures 10–12).

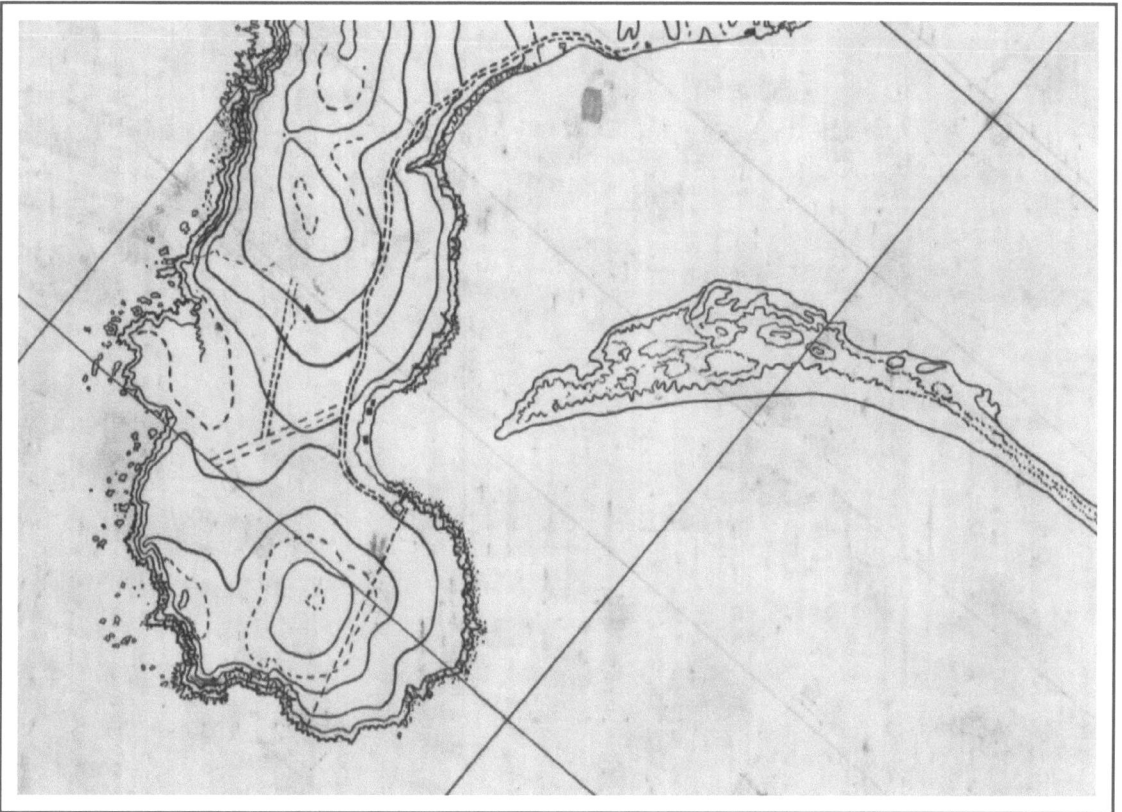

Figure 7 Three buildings, a fence, roads, and corral at the Russian landing known as Port Rumiantsev. The buildings appear as small, shaded rectangles along the east-facing cove on the east shore of Bodega Head, at the mouth of Bodega Bay. (Portion of an 1863 tracing of 1862 T-sheet no. 883; scanned by John Cloud at NARA II.)

Figure 8   1851 or 1852 drawing of Presidio Hill Station by Richard Cutts (1851–1852) showing the Presidio adobes and their setting in San Francisco.   (Photographed by author at NARA II.)

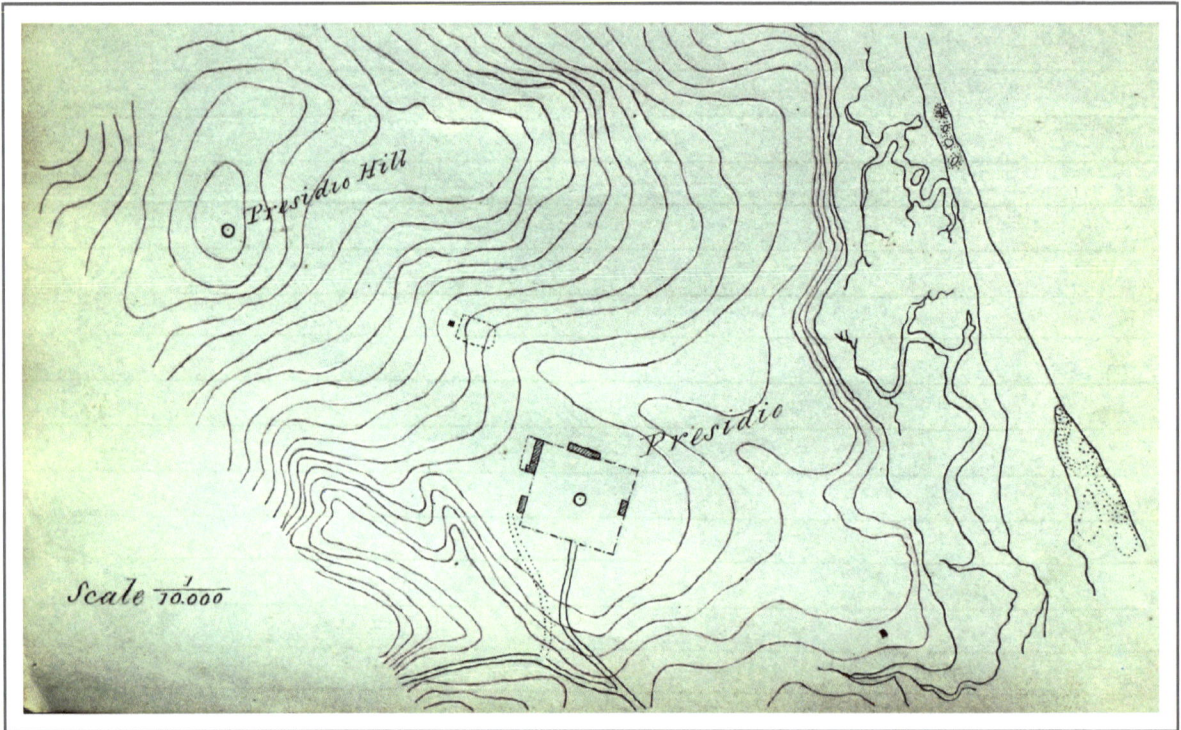

Figure 9   Map of Presidio Hill Station and its vicinity accompanying the sketch shown in Figure 8.

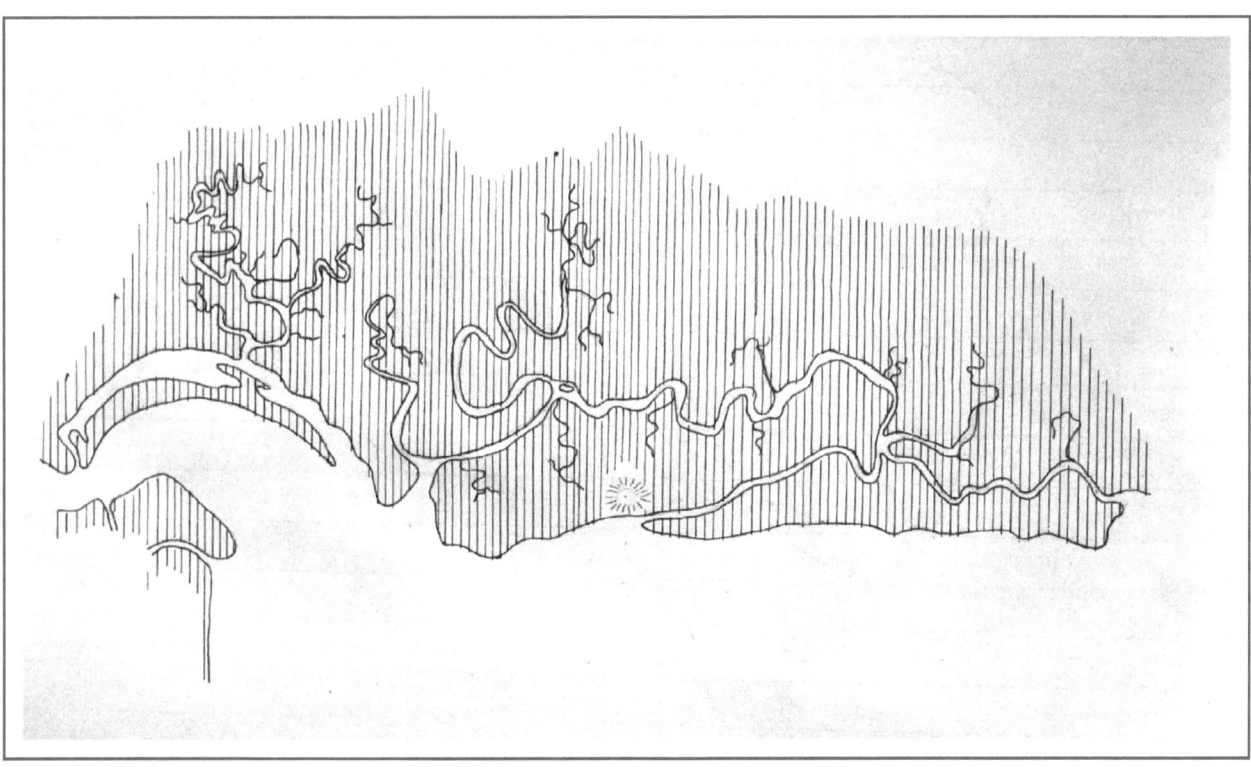

Figure 10   Map of marsh area south of San Pablo showing a mound at or near Ellis Landing (site CA-CCO-295) near the shore in the lower center of the image. The mound was chosen for Contra Costa 4 Station, but Cutts (1851–1852) recorded no description. (Photographed by author at NARA II.)

The USCS records are distinct from those of the General Land Office (GLO), the predecessor agency to the Bureau of Land Management (BLM), which mapped during the same era. GLO surveys established the township and range system across much of the West, and the agency's records overlap with the USCS near the coast (Dracup 2006). GLO records are widely incorporated into archaeological analysis in the US, though in much of California these records are sometimes superseded by Mexican land grants and derivative parcel surveys. While GLO records often include valuable information about historical landscapes, trails, and settlement, the GLO used much more expedient survey methods than the USCS.

Unlike GLO records that have been available to researchers in BLM district offices, most of the descriptive field notes and manuscript maps of the USCS remained in the agency's internal archives, libraries, and field offices for many decades, largely unexamined by archaeologists. Today many of these records are in the holdings of NARA II in College Park, Maryland. Others are housed at the National Oceanic and Atmospheric Administration (NOAA) Central Library and several regional archives. My goal in this study is to bring to light some of the more important and less accessible historical records in the USCS archives and to offer California archaeology scholars a way to research this expansive collection. Just as later surveyors used these records to reposition

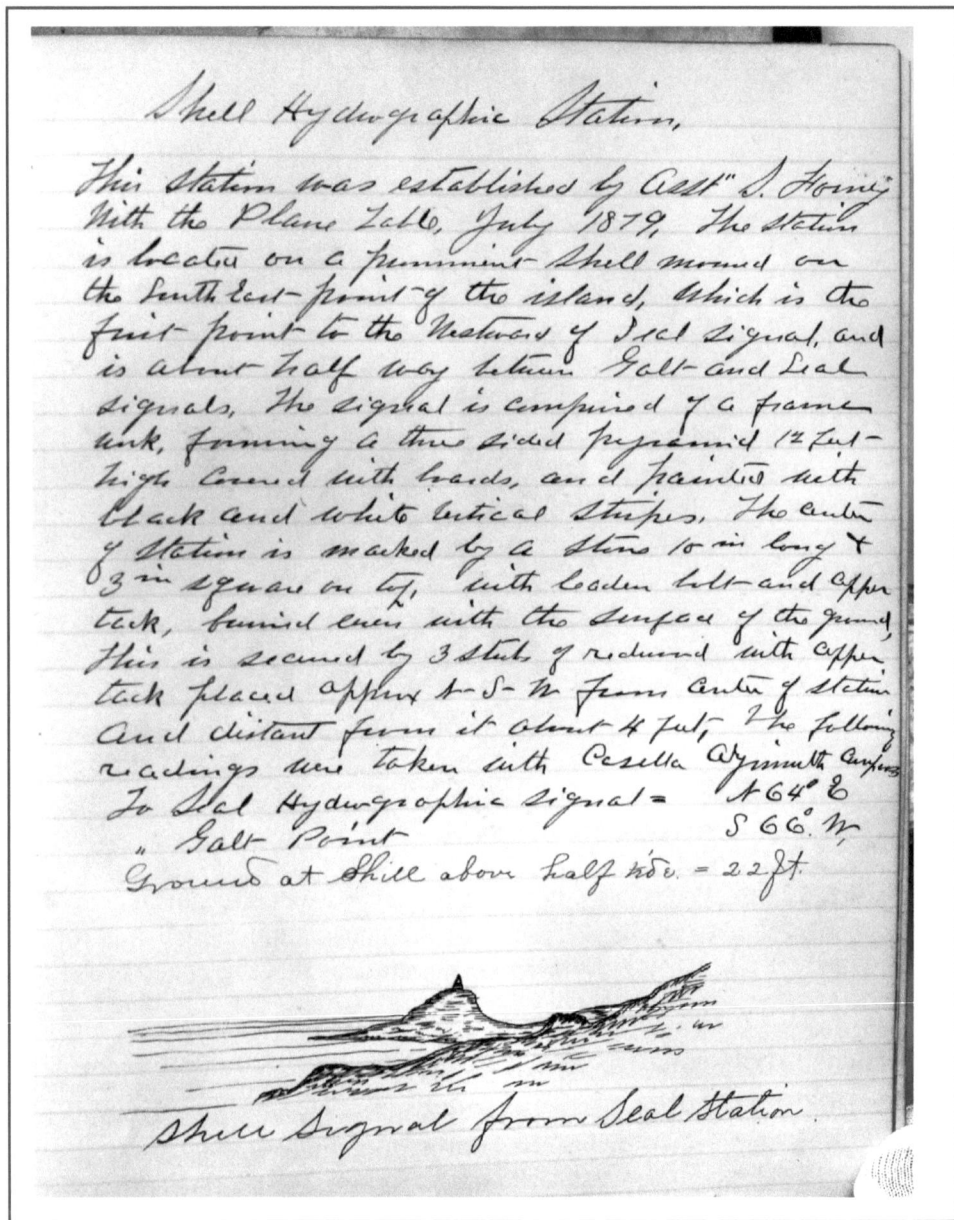

Figure 11 Page from Forney's (1879) field notebook documenting the shell mound at the present-day Shell hydrographic station (remnants recorded as site CA-SNI-74). The mound was subsequently destroyed before further recording, possibly during road construction. The station marker is a 12 ft. high pyramid tower appearing on top of the mound in the profile sketch (facing west). (Photographed by author at NARA II.)

themselves in the landscapes seen by the surveyors who left the maps and notebooks, today's archaeologists can use these records to delineate and perhaps reimagine the settings described before the transformative decades that followed. My research adds to efforts at dissemination by NOAA (2011a; 2011b; 2011c), the University of Alabama (2011), and the San Francisco Estuary Institute, among others.

Agency History

The US Coast Survey was formed in 1807 by Thomas Jefferson, who was himself an accomplished surveyor (Allen 1997). From 1878 until the 1970s it was known as the US Coast and Geodetic Survey (USCGS), and its maps, photos, and text records at the National Archives are organized under this name in Record Group 23 (Matchette 1995).

The Office of the Coast Survey continues today as a branch of NOAA's National Ocean Service (Dracup 2006). For much of the nineteenth century, the USCS was tasked with mapping the coastline and harbors of the United States for defense and economic expansion, reflecting the agency's long-term presence within the Department of the Treasury.

The accuracy of ongoing USCS surveys and the detail of their site descriptions were the outcome of the priorities of the agency's leadership. By the middle nineteenth century,

Figure 12   Portion of 1889 T-sheet no. 2014 showing Shell Mound Station at what is now Torrey Pines Golf Course in San Diego. The delta marking the station is circumscribed by a topographic contour that may represent the mound perimeter or its upper terrace margin. The ocean beach is in the lower portion of the cropped image. (Scanned by John Cloud at NARA II.)

Figure 13   The US Coast Survey brig *Fauntleroy*, used primarily by Davidson's party from 1854 to 1881 on the West Coast. Photograph by Edward Muybridge. (Photograph in possession of the author.)

the US Coast Survey was recognized internationally for its scientific research (Barnard 1858; NOAA 2011b; Slotten 1994). Their surveys observed many aspects of natural science from shipboard laboratories (Figures 13 and 14). West Coast survey teams were also tasked with documenting the history of exploration on the Pacific coast and assessing locations for fortifications and lighthouses (Cutts 1853a, 1853b; Theberge 2011).

The USCS hydrographic charts were critical to navigation in the eastern Pacific. But the USCS was not the only party conducting waterway mapping in California during the nineteenth century; portions of the coast had been charted by Cabrillo, Tebenkoff, Wilkes, Beechey, and many others. Beginning in 1849 naval officers contracted with private parties to conduct surveys of the inland waterway routes to the gold fields, and the navy charted shorelines for military bases (Delgado 2009:44; Huston 2000).

Figure 14 US Coast and Geodetic Survey ship *Active* under steam. (Courtesy of NOAA Central Library.)

Figure 15 US Coast Survey party of George Davidson at San Luis Obispo, probably 1871. (Courtesy of NOAA Central Library.)

The navy's more expedient shoreline mapping techniques differed from those of the USCS, which reflected the scientific orientation of its staff and leadership. Shorelines were also mapped by the General Land Office and other federal agencies, but none achieved a level of accuracy and attention to detail comparable to the USCS.

Alexander Bache was superintendent of the USCS from 1843 to 1865, including the years when the agency conducted key surveys of the West Coast. In a century when geographical sciences were preeminent, Bache was recognized by many as the head of the American scientific community (Slotten 1994). He served as the first president of the National Academy of Sciences and held other distinguished titles (Slotten 1994:6, 37, 136, 143). The chief surveyors with the USCS held the title of Assistant, reflecting their direct relationship to Bache in all survey matters. The letters between Bache and the assistants are part of the agency's archives. Bache, as well as many of the assistants, published numerous articles in scientific journals throughout the nineteenth century, many of them based on their findings during field research and related analysis.

Among the better-known individuals who served with the USCS on the West Coast were naturalists Louis Agassiz and William H. Dall; the painters James Whistler, Cleveland Rockwell, and James Madison Alden; and George Davidson, the preeminent geographer of the Pacific seaboard.

Davidson headed the West Coast branch of the USCS for decades, serving concurrently as an honorary professor of astronomy, geodesy, and geography at the University of California, where he ultimately became a regent (Eldredge 1915:231–232; Lewis 1954). His extensive archives are housed in the Bancroft Library at the University of California, Berkeley. Davidson was president of the California Academy of Sciences from 1871 to 1886, and he wrote several articles about the history of Pacific coast exploration (Davidson 1887; Dickie et al. 1914; Lewis 1954; NOAA 2011b; Theberge 2006:12). He documented Native American place-names extensively, and much of his ethnographic research is only recently being recognized (Cloud 2007). His 1858 *Directory for the Pacific Coast of the United States* became the first in the *Pacific Coast Pilot* series, an indispensible guide for mariners that contains much historical information. The Davidson inshore current and several mountain and shoreline features of the western states are named for him.

Davidson initially led the astronomical positioning work on the West Coast (Figure 15), but not the topography work. From 1850 to 1855 the survey's West Coast triangulation and topographic operations were headed by Richard D. Cutts, who is less well known in California but also was an accomplished, internationally recognized scientist (Byram 2005). The nephew of President James Madison, Cutts grew up hearing stories of the Lewis and Clark expedition and the War of 1812. After Georgetown College, he joined the Northeast Boundary Survey before beginning his 40 years of service with the Coast Survey. He rose to be one of the agency's leading geographers, also serving as a diplomat and brevet general in the Civil War. While in San Francisco, Cutts became a close associate of the prominent Californian Henry Halleck, and later served as aide-de-camp to the man who was Lincoln's chief general during the Civil War (Ambrose 1962:226; Theberge

2011:606–607). Cutts's brother James Madison Cutts authored the influential book *The Conquest of California and New Mexico in the Years 1846 and 1847.*

Other surveyors on the Pacific coast include William E. Greenwell, who headed the southern California office in Santa Barbara for many years, James Lawson (who assisted George Davidson), Stehman Forney, Louis Sengsteller, Benjamin A. Colonna, Augustus F. Rodgers, and William B. McMurtrie.

USCS Archaeological Research

While the value of USCS records is in the accuracy of their maps and the detailed description that accompanies them, in some cases the surveyors also conducted scientific research specific to the fields of archaeology, ethnography, and history. At least four surveyors with the USCS in California became known by later archaeologists for their archaeological observations during surveys on the Pacific coast. G. Harford collected on San Miguel Island in 1872–1873 (Moratto 1984:121; Stearns 1873) and Sub-assistant Paul Schumacher served on the Oregon and California coast prior to his better-known research for the Smithsonian (Garcia 2010). During these surveys he became familiar with Native American archaeological sites (Heizer 1978:7; Moratto 1984:121; Schumacher 1874), and this set the stage for his role in mapping sites and collecting artifacts for exhibits at the 1876 Centennial Exposition in Philadelphia. Assistant Alexander W. Chase worked with Paul Schumacher on some surveys and sometimes conducted informal archaeological and ethnographic investigations (Chase 1869a; Lyman 1991).

In a recent thesis on Schumacher, Tracy Garcia (2010) of the University of Oregon notes that Chase and Schumacher may have been in competition with regard to their archaeological work. Like Schumacher's collections, Chase's artifacts and field notes were accessioned by the Smithsonian. Chase's investigations have been researched by R. Lee Lyman (1991) and Thomas Blackburn (2005), and his biographical journals have recently been brought to light by Robert Kentta (2011) of the Confederated Tribes of Siletz Indians. Finally, William H. Dall conducted archaeological surveys in California in conjunction with the USCS, following his extensive research in Alaska (Garcia 2010). Numerous other studies by USCS researchers provided important ecological context for archaeological research at the Smithsonian as well as the California Academy of Sciences (Zwinger 1987).

There were also more casual investigations. For all surveyors, there was often idle time spent waiting for weather to clear in order to conduct surveys or travel by sea. During this time, in addition to perfecting their maps and calculations, they often explored nearby areas, sketched landscapes and people, and wrote journal entries and letters. Whistler, McMurtrie, Rockwell, Alden, Chase, and others each left sketches, journals, correspondence, drawings, or paintings they made while in the field. These records are in the Bancroft Library, the California Historical Society collections, the Oregon History Center, and other US archives (Holland 1997; Hughes 2002; Monroe 1959; Stenzel 1972, 1975). The NOAA website has an extensive history section with biographies of several of the surveyors and journal transcripts of individuals who worked in California and elsewhere (NOAA 2011b; Theberge 2011).

Chapter 2

SITUATED CULTURAL DESCRIPTION:
CALIFORNIA T-SHEETS AND FIELD NOTEBOOKS

Although West Coast scholars are familiar with the some of the published maps and reports of the USCS, and copies of manuscript topographic sheets, known as "T-sheets," have occasionally been examined by researchers for information about historic towns, trails, and other features, the field notebooks and other records prepared in conjunction with the manuscript maps have largely been unavailable as a source of historical and archaeological data. And the vast majority of T-sheets have not yet been examined for historical and archaeological data. Used together, the maps and notes hold vast information relevant to archaeology, history, architectural studies, and related topics.

The maps the USCS made and the reports that went with them are increasingly cited in studies of historical ecology and other fields (Engstrom 2006; Perroy et al. 2012; Shalowitz 1964). The San Francisco Estuary Institute has developed innovative online GIS tools for some California USCS maps (Grossinger et al. 2011; San Francisco Estuary Institute 2012). Reproductions of several USCS manuscript maps are held in university libraries and regional historical societies, though the low resolution of these reproductions of the ink and pencil maps often leaves out many details. Dr. John Cloud and Captain Albert Theberge of the NOAA Central Library have led efforts to make high-resolution color images of USCS manuscript maps available, but the images are so large that the scans are time consuming to produce, requiring much NARA or NOAA staff time. Fortunately, the NOAA Maritime Heritage Program is initiating efforts to put online those T-sheets that have been scanned in color at high resolution as part of their Maritime Cultural Landscapes initiative (Cloud 2013). The field notebooks are less accessible than the maps, and the delicate bound volumes cannot be photocopied. It may be several years before the majority of the USCS manuscript maps and notes are available digitally from NARA II holdings in color and at high resolution.

Earlier examples of the use of USCS maps in historical studies generally involve research on specific topics, though regional studies such as Dicken's (1961) *Pioneer Trails of the Oregon Coast* incorporated data from numerous manuscript T-sheet tracings on file with the Oregon Historical Society. I first presented findings from USCS archival research in Oregon in 1999, research that ultimately led to a paper on Lewis and Clark's Fort Clatsop (Byram 2005). In a recent issue of the *Journal of San Diego History*, Trent and Seymour (2010) explain that the discovery of an 1856 sketch by surveyor William B. McMurtrie in the holdings of the Bancroft Library led to research on the Serra palm (planted by Junipero Serra) in Old Town San Diego. Researchers in several California cities have consulted T-sheet tracings or photocopies in local libraries, such as the copy of T-sheet no. 444 showing Santa Cruz in 1853 in the holdings of the Santa Cruz public library, and multiple T-sheets of San Francisco showing wharf development (Delgado 2009:84; Hayes 2007:106) and possible shell mounds (Banks 1981). Historic landscape studies of Presidio San Francisco have relied on maps that appear to be derived from USCS T-sheets from the 1850s as evidence of architecture and plaza layout (Wolfram 2010:15). Studies of the Spanish Fort Guijarros (Ballast Point) at San Diego Bay reference USCS T-sheets and charts (May 1995). Fort Ross researchers (California Department of Parks and Recreation 2004) reference a copy of T-sheet no. 1457 (1876) on file at the Bancroft Library in delineating historical structure locations. Navy archaeologist Steve Schwartz (2010, 2012a, 2012b) has used T-sheets scanned at NARA II for San Nicolas Island research. While with the USCGS, George Davidson used the agency's maps in historical research; for example, he used a Coast Survey map overlaid onto the map made by Sir Francis Drake (Davidson 1887:156) in order to conclude that the Marin County cove known as Drake's Bay was the likely landfall of the *Golden Hinde* in 1579, and he referenced USCS topographic mapping several times in this and other reports.

Field notebooks of the USCS have rarely been used in historical or archaeological studies in California. Historian Dewey Livingston's (2004) scanning and transcription of selected pages from Channel Islands USCS and USCGS field notebooks is one example. Additionally, modern survey historians (e.g., Pettley 1998) have used these records to retrace earlier positions, much as the field notes from earlier surveys were used in subsequent USCS and USCGS surveys through the early twentieth century.

Triangulation and Topographic Mapping

Early in his tenure with the USCS, Alexander Bache saw the need for accurate and detailed topographic sheets as a basis for consistent nautical chart accuracy and to provide shoreline context for navigation (NOAA 2011a; Slotten 1994). The key to these maps was instrument survey using triangulation, as well as the use of large-format plane table mapping in the field. Nineteenth-century surveyors triangulated using optical instruments that measured angles and distances. Triangulation required use of a theodolite with a telescope and rotating vernier for extremely accurate angle measurement to determine distances using trigonometric computations. Independently, latitude and longitude coordinates were obtained for several locations using astronomical observations and chronometers.

Triangulation involves the precise placement of baselines of known length and the positioning of mapping stations or signals in line of sight from baseline endpoints and other subsequent mapping stations. Using accurate angle measurement, mapping stations were sighted and marked, then occupied by the surveyor and instrument as the mapping continued across the landscape. With a large theodolite, the precise location of a point miles from the measured baseline is possible through triangulation (Yu 1995). The first triangulation on the West Coast was performed by the USCS using a baseline set at Presidio San Francisco in 1851 and the second was at Pulgas, near Palo Alto (Dracup 2006). The accuracy of the earliest California surveys was attested to some 80 years later by USCGS Captain T. J. Maher (1933) who wrote:

> In 1853 the Pulgas Base, lying about 35 miles southward of San Francisco, was measured by the party of R. D. Cutts ... Persistence and attention to detail produced an accuracy comparable to what we obtain today.
>
> The triangulation from the Pulgas Base gave a length to the Yolo Base which exceeded its true length by 0.35 meter, a difference which is equivalent to about 1/50,000 of the actual length.

The surveys were so accurate that resurvey was feasible after the 1906 San Francisco earthquake to determine the extent of crustal deformation in several areas (Dracup 2006; Hayford and Baldwin 1908). Given this level of accuracy, positions recorded for mapped archaeological and historical features in the nineteenth century are nearly as accurate as those recorded with modern mapping methods, though accuracy decreases for features more distant from survey stations.

During triangulation, a "Descriptions of Stations" notebook was used to record the setting of the mapping position and nearby features in sufficient detail to allow future surveyors to locate the monument again. In Cutts's (1871) *Memoranda Relating to the Field-Work of the Secondary Triangulation*, he described the selection of triangulation stations:

> The sweep of the horizon, or the area to be surveyed, with a view to the easy determination of intermediate stations, and of light-houses, spires, chimneys, or other prominent objects not more than two or three miles apart, for the special use of the plane table and hydrographical parties.

These notebooks included a "description, and generally a sketch of each triangulation-point, showing the manner in which it has been marked, and the bearings and distances of any objects near at hand, by which its location can be found"; landmarks could include "prominent chimneys, the apex of gables of buildings, flag-staffs, lone trees," etc. (Cutts 1878:4). Astronomical stations and hydrographic stations were also recorded in these notebooks. In later years geodetic positions were described in inland settings, though some inland peaks were visited as early as 1860 for long-distance triangulation (Davidson 1860).

Symbol conventions changed, but because the staff of the agency was small and in close communication, symbols were frequently standardized. Topographic map standards appeared in both internal and published agency documents (Harrison 1867; Hergesheimer 1881; Shalowitz 1964:197). An 1852 map of Sausalito Station (Figure 16) incorporates several standard conventions. Topographic contour lines are in red, while all other drawing is black. Solid rectangles are roofed structures, and open rectangles are structures lacking roofs, such as wharves and corrals (though not shown on this map, open-sided roofed structures or unimproved storage buildings were sometimes marked with lines crossing from opposite corners to form an X). Fence lines are dashed; cloud-like shapes are trees and shrubs.

Hachures show embankments, including mound perimeters, and solid lines portray streams. On the right side a beach is indicated by stippling and all along the shoreline a dotted line reflects an intertidal position, possibly mean tide level. The survey station Sausalito appears as an open circle near the shoreline in the lower center of the map. On this map, the label "Sausalito" refers to the town, and the label "Richardson" identifies the rancho to the northwest.

Unlike cadastral surveyors, the USCS did not attempt to document the full extent of US settlement across the land. The goal in documenting a station with a map was to choose landmarks that were "intervisible," or shared a line of sight, and that were relatively stable for later relocation. In some areas only trees and topography were available, but as settlement increased, structures of various kinds, roads, fence lines, and other features were depicted on topographic sheets and station maps in notebooks. The maps clearly differentiate plowed fields and orchards from native vegetation, and landscape types, from intertidal beach to low and high marsh, prairie, and forested upland, are all evident. Along the ocean shore and navigable tidewaters, shoals, kelp beds, and rock hazards are often depicted, along with buoys and other channel or harbor markers. Both manuscript charts and field notebooks were cataloged at regional offices and/or the central library in Washington, DC. These were archived for the use of future surveyors, who often took original or hand-traced duplicates of these records into the field.

NOAA Central Library historian John Cloud has researched the changing methods of map preparation by the USCS. He notes that

> Early US Coast Survey-published engraved charts used hachures for land topography, but as early as 1844 (after A. D. Bache became Superintendent) the Survey's original manuscript maps, called t-sheets ("t" for topography) began incorporating contours for topography, almost always in red ink, a color which was from that time forward reserved for contours. In some early cases both hachures and contours were used together on the t-sheets, but eventually pure contouring in red became standard on the t-sheets. (Cloud 2008)

Topographic contouring consisting of elevation-specific lines was used more frequently than hatching to show elevation changes in field notebooks as well. In some cases these contour lines appeared at finer intervals in Descriptions of Stations notebooks than on the T-sheets (Figure 17), and in other cases the notebook maps are simply tracings of portions of T-sheets.

Research with the USCS Collection at NARA II

The scale of T-sheets is often 1:10,000 or 1:20,000. Station maps in field notebooks are often at the same scale or smaller. In some cases the notebook maps are simply traced from portions of the T-sheets, but the tracings often include additional information about the area of the station. On both types of survey maps, structures are often exaggerated slightly in scale to reveal shape and distinctive features. This is not the case for USCS urban-area maps or other depictions at comparable levels of detail. An example of enlarged structures is Greenwell's 1853 map of Santa Monica Station and Santa Monica Canyon (Figure 18) showing the Ysidro Reyes adobe and what is likely the nearby Marquez adobe. The exaggerated size allowed Greenwell to depict the distinctive architecture of the Reyes adobe. The shallow U-shape of the structure does not appear on Chase's more proportionally accurate 1875 map of the building (Figure 19), which shows only a small rectangle labeled as a ruin.

USCS hydrographic charts are well known for their regularly spaced numerals that show nearshore basin depth in feet or fathoms for vessel navigation. This was a separate task of the agency following triangulation and topographic mapping that set survey markers used during the hydrographic surveys.

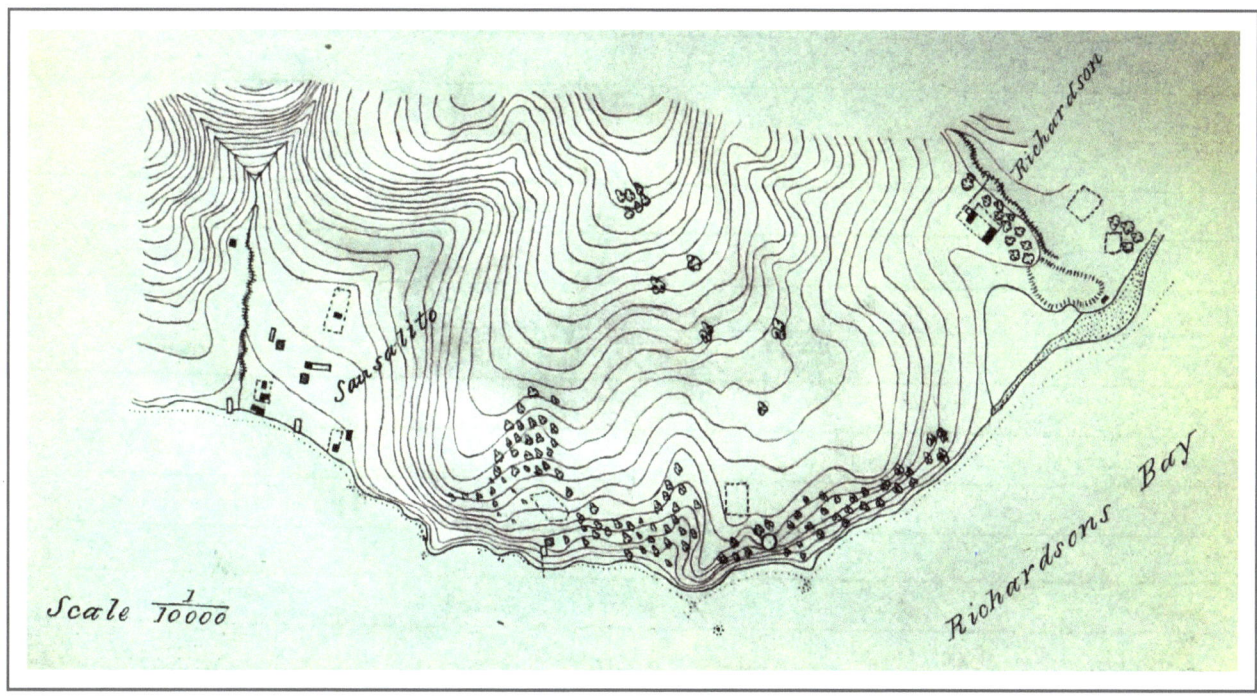

Figure 16   Map of Sausalito Station by Richard D. Cutts (1851–1852).   (Photographed by author at NARA II.)

Most of the early survey markers set by the USCS were not permanent, though a durable marker was often buried below the surface for relocation by later surveyors. California survey marking signage was in both English and Spanish, especially in the southern part of the state. During the twentieth century these positions were typically relocated and the markers replaced with the more permanent concrete markers and brass caps that many of us today are familiar with. In the course of these revisits, the positions of most California survey stations were confirmed and recorded, appearing in later reports.

Latitude and longitude positions for 728 southern California triangulation stations appear in the 1904 USCGS annual report (Baldwin 1904), with brief station descriptions for each. Positions and descriptions for 1,817 stations were included in the 1910 USCGS annual report (Duvall and Baldwin 1911) for California north of Monterey Bay. Approximately 75% of these stations are described in the two annual reports, though often with less detail than in field notebooks. These reports also include triangulation maps that allow identification of primary and secondary stations in a given survey area. Most stations also appear on T-sheets for a given area. The field notes (entitled "Descriptions of Stations" or "Descriptions of Signals") for stations established by 1895 are in 122 bound volumes at NARA II, some containing notes from multiple surveys and some being duplicates. These are cataloged in the GA Series of Record Group 23. The name of the surveyor and the initial date the station was recorded can be used to locate the field notebook. In addition there are six California volumes in the GAR series. Relevant records on NARA microfilm include numerous reels of correspondence, much of this between Bache and the assistants in the field (Bache 1843–1865). Copies of some field notes are also in the holdings of the Bancroft Library (George Davidson collection) and the Oregon History Center (Cleveland Rockwell collection).

In the cartographic records at NARA II there are approximately 370 T-sheets for the California coast dating between 1850 and 1895. Several more T-sheets date between 1895 and 1940. Figure 20 is an example of one page in the NARA II T-sheet index. Scans of other California T-sheet index pages for the period 1850–1895 appear in the appendix to this volume. A PDF of the entire index is likely to be accessible online at the NOAA website in the near future. For some areas, such as San Francisco Bay, there were numerous surveys for a given location, but in other cases, such as San Diego, the T-sheets drawn in the 1850s served as the primary topographic base map for charts until a more detailed series was produced in 1887. A typical T-sheet might represent a portion of the coastline 10 miles long and extend inland 2 miles or more, often to the top of prominent ridge lines.

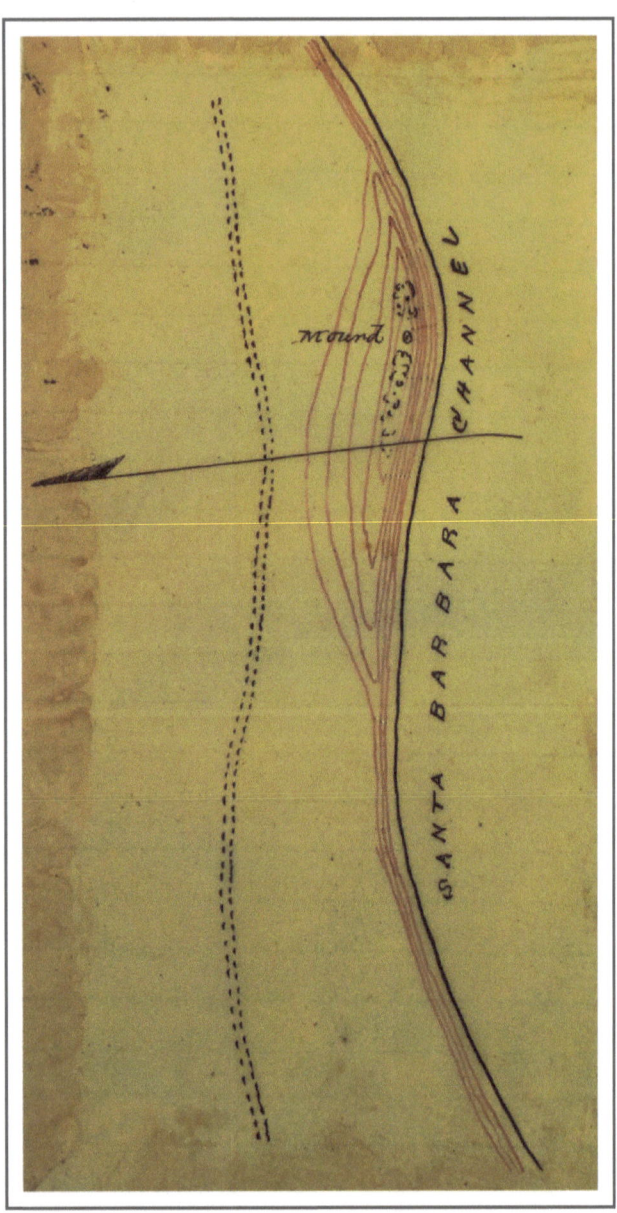

Figure 17 Mound Station near Loon Point, Santa Barbara County (Greenwell 1862–1863). (Photographed by author at NARA II.)

Black and white photographic negatives of T-sheets are on file at NARA II, but large-scale color digital images are not available for most sheets. In most cases only the negatives are accessible to researchers,

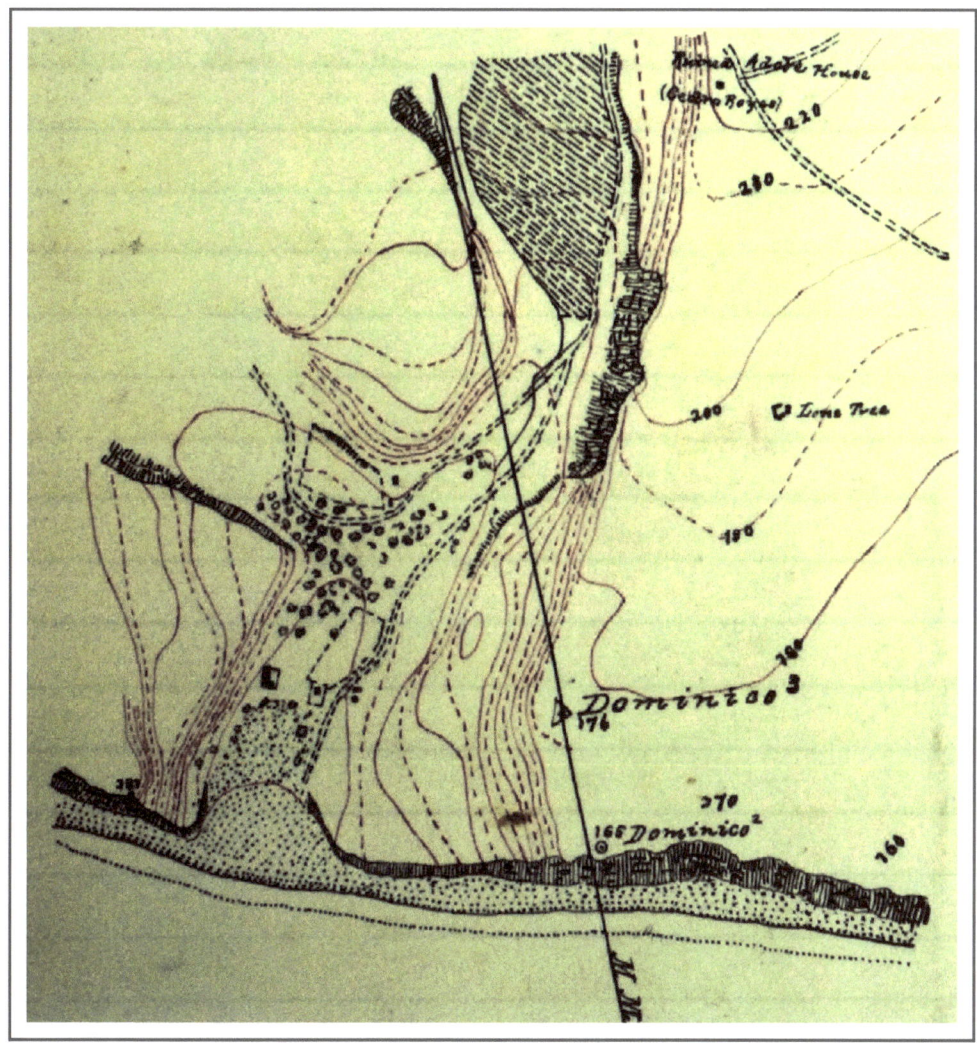

Figure 18   Ruins of the Cedro (Ysidro) Reyes adobe in Santa Monica and other features in Santa Monica Canyon (Chase 1875). (Photographed by author at NARA II.)

and not all negatives are present in these files (some are likely misfiled). An example of a scan from a negative is the portion of T-sheet no. 360 shown in Figure 21. NOAA researchers have scanned a fraction of the nineteenth-century T-sheets in color at high resolution (e.g., Figures 5 and 12), but the electronic distribution of these has been limited because file size is typically 100 megabytes or more per map image.

Because inverted scanning of fragile bound volumes can be destructive, it is prohibited at NARA II. For this study, digital photography was used to reproduce notebook pages or portions thereof, including text as well as maps. I used a Nikon D80 SLR camera with a 10 megapixel CCD image sensor and a 50 mm lens. Images were captured using natural light provided by large windows in the text records room, and a photo stand was used to position the camera at least 2 ft. (0.6 m) from the notebook page. The 50 mm lens greatly limits distortion at the margins of the images. A scale rule was included with photos of each volume to allow map scale conversions based on the ratios shown on most of the maps. However, images imported into GIS software can also be scaled as they are registered (i.e., tied to fixed positions) with a USGS topographic map layer (Tripcevich and Byram 2013).

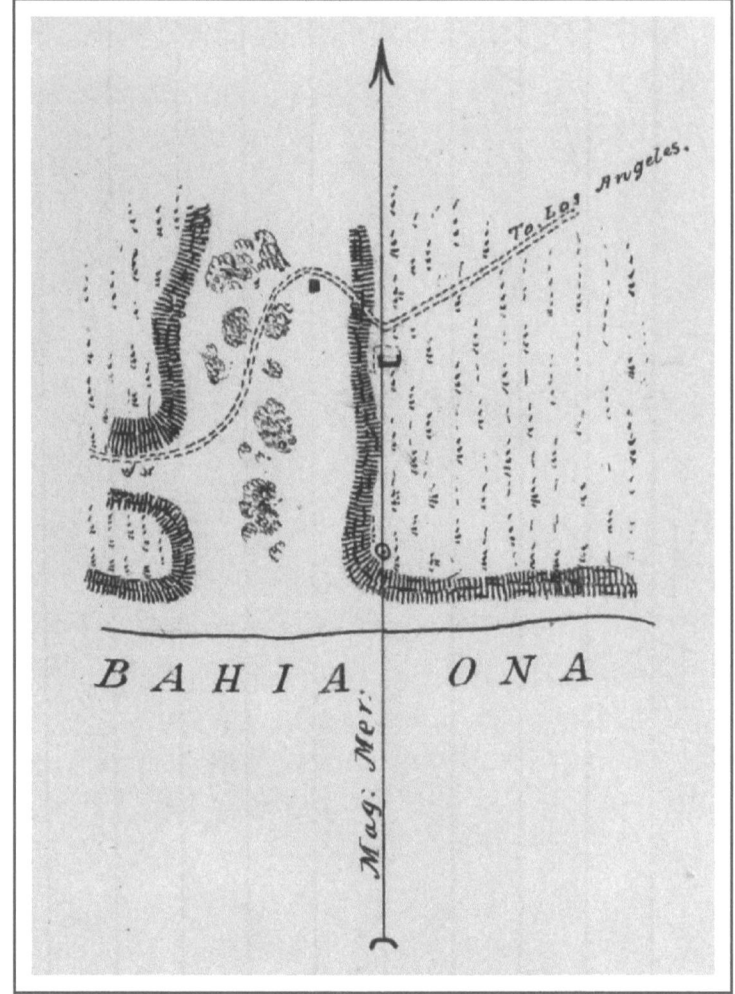

Figure 19 Greenwell's (1853–1856) sketch map of Santa Monica Station and setting, not to scale. (Photographed by author at NARA II.)

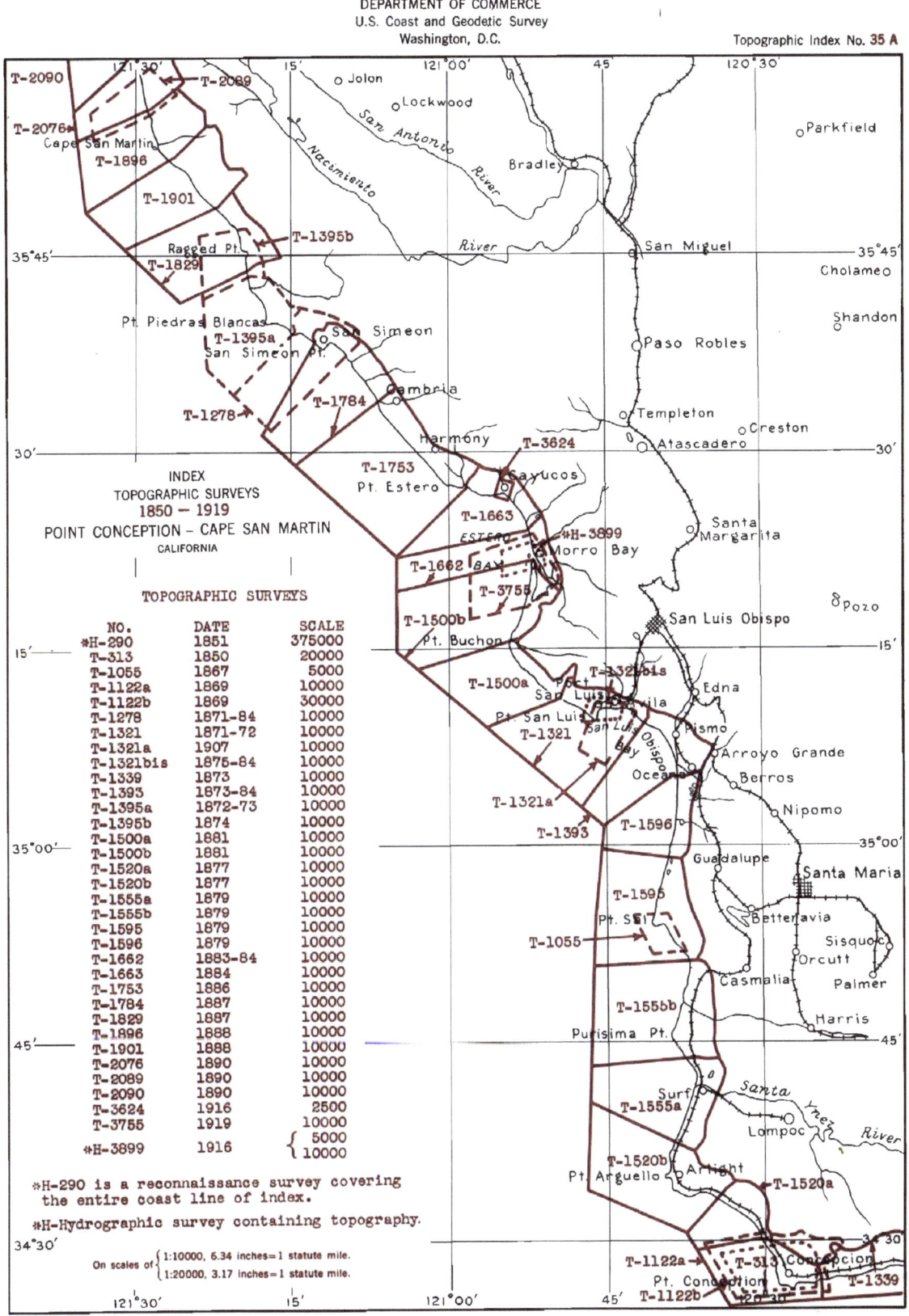

Figure 20 Page from USCGS T-sheet index at NARA II. All North American topographic and hydrographic sheets in the holdings of NARA II are catalogued in this volume. (Courtesy of NOAA Central Library.)

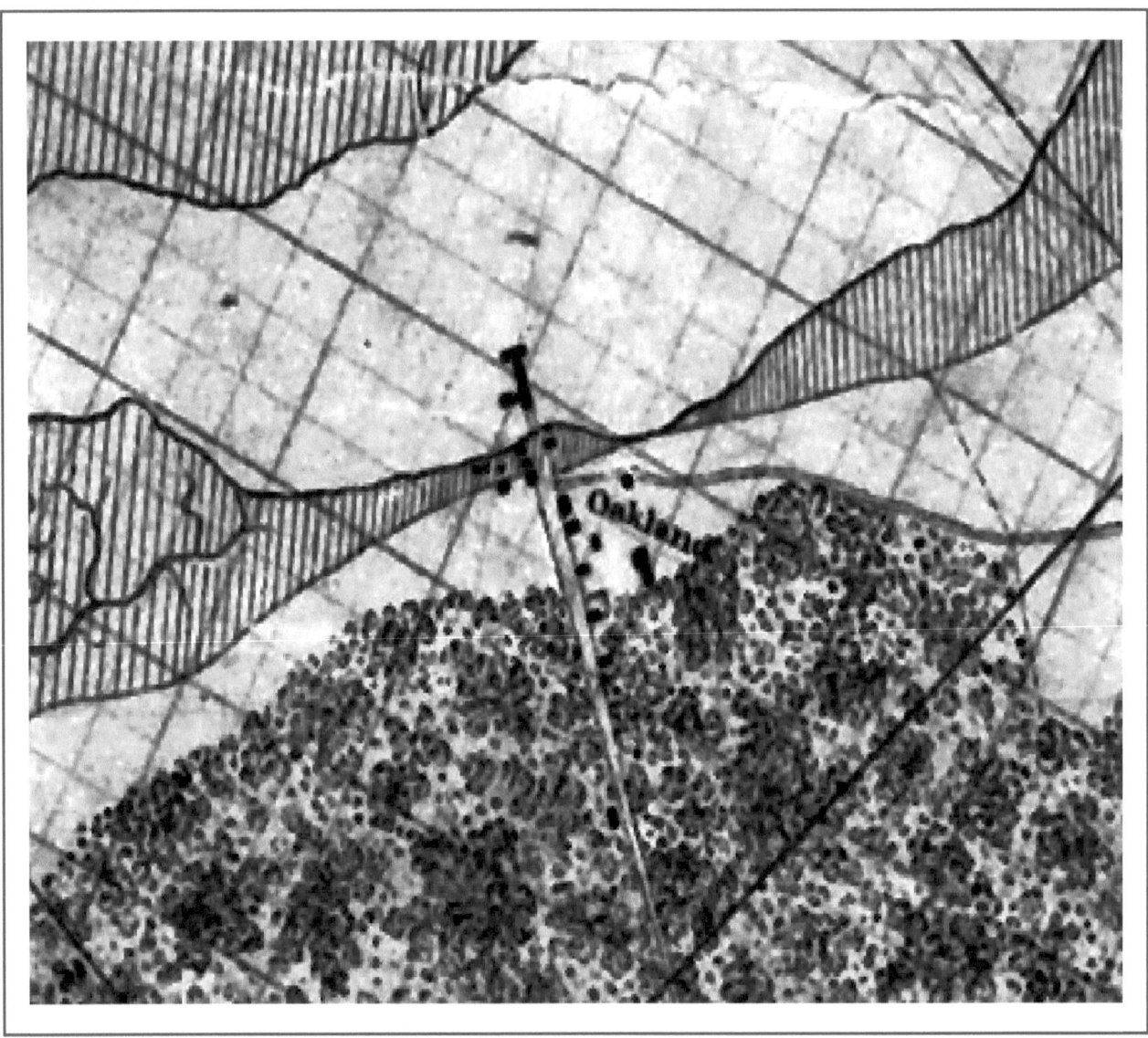

Figure 21   Portion of T-sheet no. 360 showing Oakland, California, in 1852 when oak woodlands were far more expansive than city streets in the lowlands near San Antonio Creek tidal channel.   (Inverted photo of black-and-white negative taken by author at NARA II.)

Chapter 3
Maps, Notes, and Sketches in Archaeological Interpretation: Colonial Sites

Coastal California archaeological and historical sites mapped by the US Coast Survey in the nineteenth century include a wide range of site types. To illustrate the collection, I discuss several examples grouped into nonexclusive categories. This chapter focuses on colonial sites, including much of the infrastructure the USCS was tasked with documenting. Chapter 4 addresses Native American sites, many of which were mapped because of their distinctive topography or as visual reference points for survey marker plotting.

Six categories of colonial sites or site complexes are outlined. Cities and towns include areas of concentrated residence. Landings are locations on the coast where wharves, docks, or other shipping facilities were constructed, or where ships anchored nearby and used beach landings for the transport of goods or people. Industrial sites include facilities such as lumber mills, canneries, lime kilns, smelters, mines, and tanneries. Shipwrecks are locations where the wreckage of vessels came to rest, at least temporarily. Fortifications include presidios and other military bases of varying scale. Finally, ranchos, adobes and other dwellings are residences associated with Spanish, Mexican, Californio, US, and Native American habitation, often involving livestock structures and pastures, orchards, vineyards, and crop rows. Whereas cities and towns were often mapped as a geographical unit with little or no description of most structures, ranchos and adobes were typically identified with a particular owner, family, or group. Dwellings of named individuals of historical significance are also included in this category.

Cities and Towns

The USCS mapped and described numerous cities and towns on the coast and inland tidewater shores of California. In most cases there are other archival and published maps of these communities, but USCS records offer much to archaeologists investigating early town construction. Two of the most well-known published USCS maps for California are the city maps of San Francisco (T-sheets nos. 352 and 627, 1853 and 1857) and Santa Barbara (T-sheet no. 1229a, 1870; see also Harrison 1853). These cities were first mapped after they had grown substantially. In contrast, Oakland was mapped by the USCS in 1852 when it had a single wharf, two streets, and 18 buildings (Figure 21). Other examples of places that underwent rapid town development during the 1850s through 1870s, after the Coast Survey had completed initial maps of these areas, are Sausalito (Figure 16), Redwood City,

Benicia, Pittsburgh, Vallejo, Eureka, Mendocino, Santa Cruz, Ventura, Santa Monica (Figure 18), Wilmington, and San Diego.

In more slowly urbanizing areas such as San Diego, topography was not updated for decades, though hydrographic charts were updated to show changes in the bay. Portions of coastal cities extending to more inland areas were not regularly mapped except during later USCGS geodetic surveys.

In Cutts's 1852 map of Sausalito Station (Figure 16), the older portion of the town where ships docked to take on fresh water is in the left half of the map. Only the Richardson Rancho is present in what is now the northern portion of the town fronting Richardson Bay. On the T-sheet showing Oakland in 1852 (Figure 21), the town has barely begun to enter a vast forest of oaks and other trees that covered the surrounding lowlands. Later USCS maps show that over the next 10 years, the city expanded through much of this woodland. The forest undoubtedly supplied firewood, game, and forage for pigs and goats, but its presence was relatively short lived as the settlement became a city in only a few years.

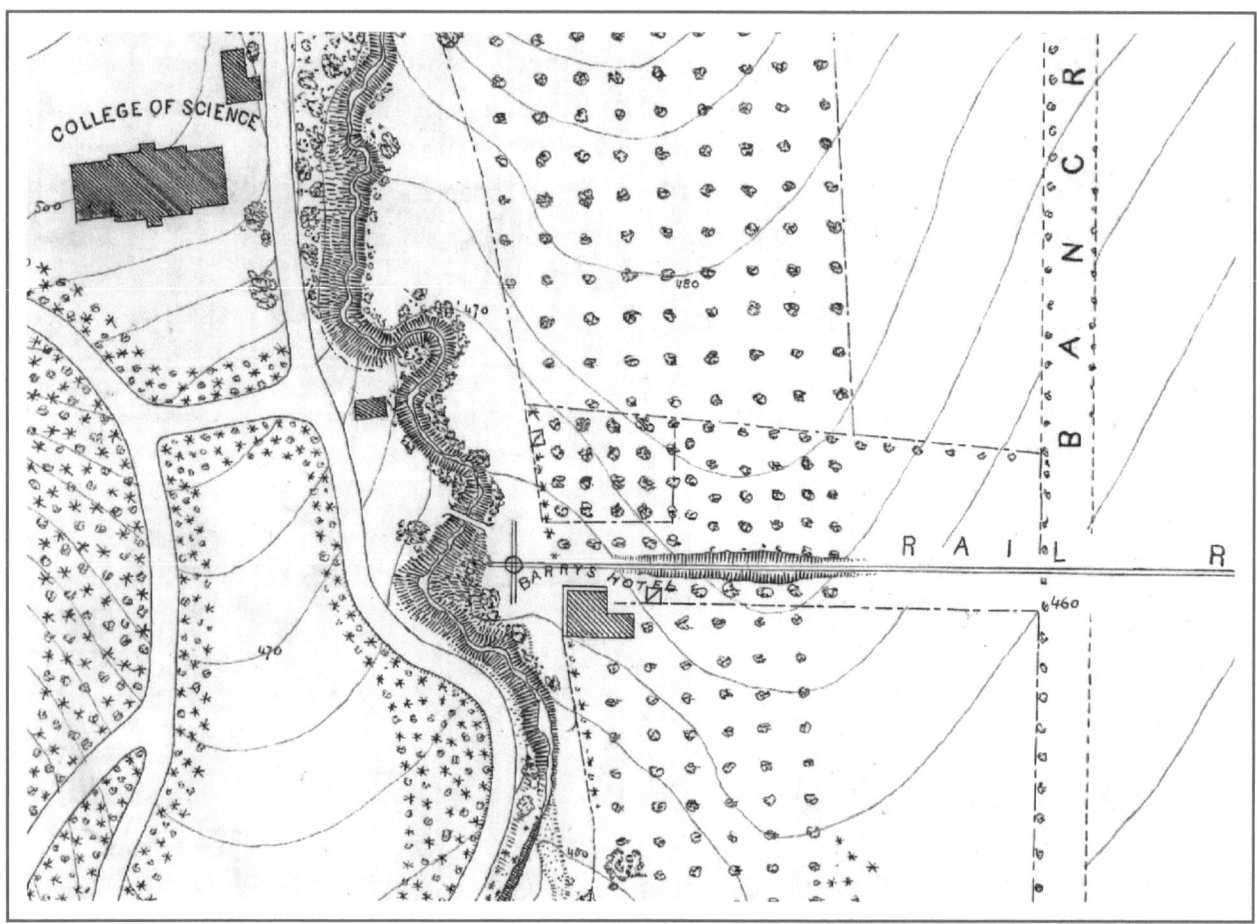

Figure 22   Portion of T-sheet no. 1622b depicting the UC Berkeley campus in 1873. Sproul Plaza now covers the location of Barry's Hotel and the Oakland trolley turnaround. (Scanned by John Cloud at NARA II.)

A number of town settings are depicted in detail in USCS records, such as mission compounds, parks, and market squares. One of the most detailed groomed landscape setting maps made by the USCS is Cleveland Rockwell's 1873 depiction of the University of California campus in Berkeley (Figure 22). Sproul Plaza has a storied history on the UC Berkeley campus as a center of student gatherings. The 1873 USCS map shows that from the earliest years of the campus this location was a gathering place for people associated with the university. Today the circle in the brickwork at the northern end of upper Sproul Plaza, near Sather Gate, represents the former turnaround for the street car that brought professors, staff, and students to the university from the Oakland neighborhoods where many lived (Wallenburg 2002). Only a few feet southwest of the circle, the wraparound porch of nearby Barry's Hotel was likely a gathering place where people awaited the arrival of the horse-drawn trolley at what was then the terminus of Choate Street. A narrow trackway had been cut through the tree-covered knoll south of the turnaround, but the street widened where it met Bancroft to the south. Surrounded by orchards that cloaked two outbuildings (possibly privies), Barry's Hotel may have offered the nearest dining to the campus community. Visiting scholars and prospective students likely stayed there. Soon after the Rockwell map was made, the street was widened and paved, and given its current name. Other hotels and commercial establishments rose up in what is now the Telegraph Avenue district (Wallenburg 2002), but the street car terminus and Barry's Hotel appear to have been the beginnings of a gathering area at this early campus-commercial interface. Sanborn Company fire insurance maps show that this block held a sequence of restaurants and stores until it was acquired by the university in the 1960s for the construction of Sproul Hall and other campus buildings.

Landings

The USCS mapped and described a wide array of embarcaderos, landings, wharves, and harbors beginning in the early 1850s. Prior to rail development, these were the primary interface between colonial transportation and local infrastructure. Some were associated with the aforementioned cities and towns, but even more common were landings that led to residential communities or agricultural or industrial sites in nearby uplands and valleys. Several of these landings later became part of larger communities, such as Old San Pedro in Los Angeles County. Others were abandoned after lumber shipping declined or railroads provided inland connections. This includes several of the "doghole" ports and lumber chutes (Haugan 2005) on the northern California coast mapped by the USCS (Figure 23). Archaeological remnants of some landings have been preserved, particularly in coastal state parks or beneath fill in urban and industrial areas such as the San Francisco waterfront (Delgado 2009).

In central California the USCS mapped several ports and landings in San Francisco Bay, as well as the bays of San Pablo, Suisun, Monterey, Tomales, and Bodega. In southern California USCS maps depict numerous small landings and anchorages in varying detail (e.g., Figure 5). Several south coast landings were heavily damaged by a tsunami on Nov. 22, 1878, after initial USCS mapping (Blank 2009; San Luis Obispo Tribune 1878).

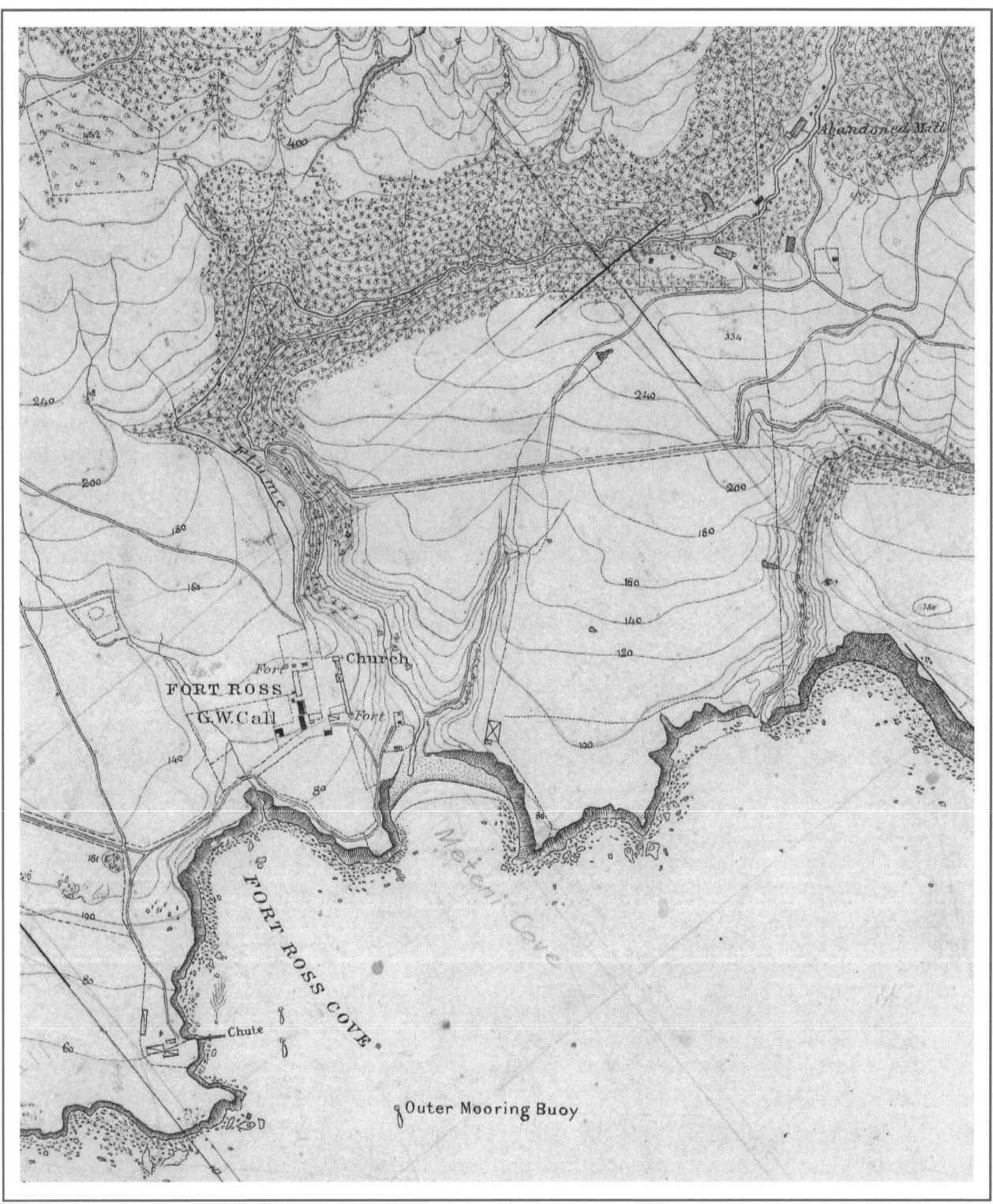

Figure 23 Portion of 1878 T-sheet no. 1457 (Fort Ross to Salt Point) by Louis Sengteller, showing the G. W. Call Ranch at Fort Ross. Some Russian structures are still present and the Russian orchard is shown in the upper left, but several new buildings have been erected and the windmills and Native American residences are gone. An abandoned lumber mill is identified in the upper right corner. Wood from this mill may have been transported through the flume and reached ships via the chute at Fort Ross Cove, one of many "doghole ports" on the California coast. (Scanned by John Cloud at NARA II.)

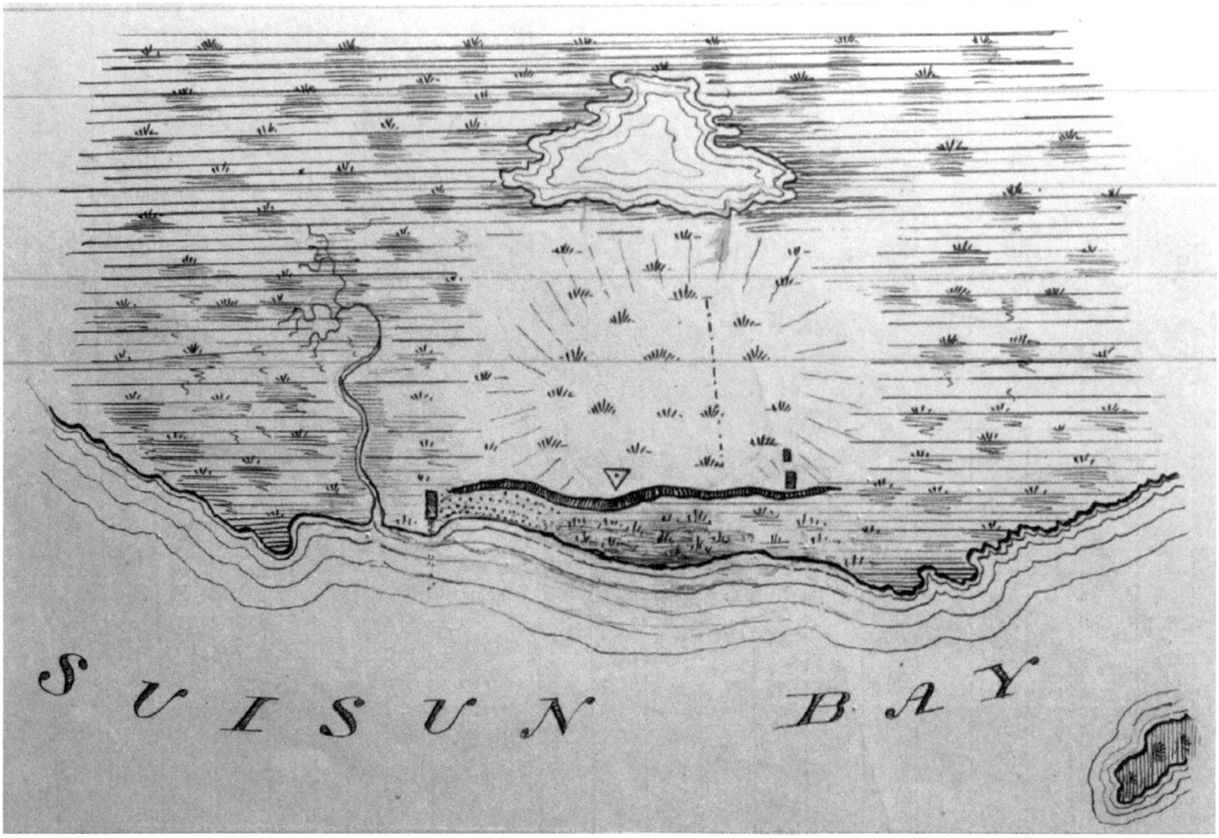

Figure 24 Map of Seal Bluff Landing at Suisun Bay by Greenwell (1866). (Photographed by author at NARA II.)

Figure 25 Seal Bluff Landing at Suisun Bay, drawn by Greenwell (1866). Note survey station marker on bluff near eroding bank. (Photographed by author at NARA II.)

Seal Bluff Landing (Figures 24 and 25) in Suisun Bay was drawn in detail by William Greenwell in 1866 after initially being described by James Lawson (1864), along with several other landings in the area. An "old warehouse" and dwelling are depicted in Greenwell's drawing and map. This was a shipping facility for wheat and other agricultural products from the area. Historical accounts note the construction of a warehouse there in 1868, but the USCS records indicate the landing was used well before then. A decade later, surveyor G. Bradford (1878) observed that because of bank erosion the warehouse (east building) had been removed and the house (west building) had been moved back. In subsequent years this waterfront grew as an integral part of the Bay Point community, which in 1931 was renamed Port Chicago. Today Port Chicago Landing is a national memorial within the Concord Naval Weapons Station. The location is known for being the site of the largest homeland disaster in World War II, when 320 men were killed in a massive explosion. The majority of these men were African American, and the responding strike by survivors is considered a key development in US military integration (Port Chicago National Memorial 2011). The USCS maps and field notes illustrate the landing's early US-period history and possibly an important Native American component as well, as addressed below.

Fishing communities and coastal whaling stations were often established by the shore, where vessels could be hauled out or anchored and the catch processed (May 1985; Scofield 1954). The USCS mapped and described several landings at fishermen's huts or cabins on the California coast, particularly in the southern part of the state. Some likely depict early Chinese junk fishing, such as Chino Station (Forney 1879) on San Nicolas Island. The mapped location corresponds to historical archaeological site AB-22 (temporary number), where Chinese ceramics are present. The date of origin for this site has not been established archaeologically, but USCS records indicate that it was in use by the 1870s. At Fisherman's Point Station in San Diego Bay, Rodgers (1887b) noted the presence of several fishermen's huts north of the station. This location corresponds to a long-standing Chinese fishing community in the area known as Roseville (Lee 2010).

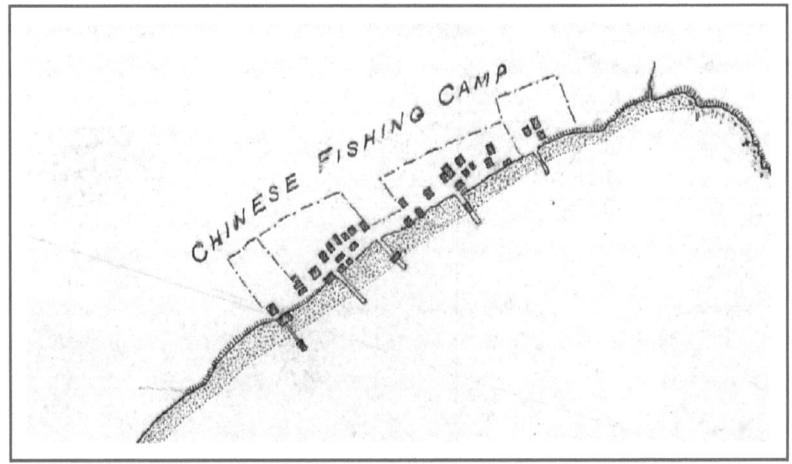

Figure 26   Portion of T-sheet no. 2445 (1898), Point Richmond to Penole Point, showing the Chinese fishing community in Contra Costa County near Point Molate. (NARA II scan courtesy of NOAA Central Library.)

Because of laws against East Asian immigration that restricted fishing, most Chinese fishing communities were abandoned by 1912. The 1898 USCS map of the Chinese fishing camp near Point Molate in San Francisco Bay (Figure 26) is a rare example of a map showing the nineteenth-century layout of one of these villages. Features associated with this village were recorded as archaeological site CA-CCO-506-H by Chavez and Holson (1985; see also Analytical Environmental Services 2009:3.6-1).

The village layout appears on the 1898 T-sheet no. 2445, Point Richmond to Penole Point. While 18 structures and four wharves appear on the 1915 US Geological Survey map of the village (drawn at a 30-minute scale), the 1898 USCGS manuscript map shows the full 30 structures and five wharves that correspond to historical accounts and photos from the years when the community was active. The layout suggests the village was divided into four areas that may have been associated with corporate groups.

At Point San Luis near San Luis Obispo, surveyor Louis Sengteller (1871) documented the structures of a Portuguese whaling company that had been established there in 1868 (Scofield 1954). During this early phase the whalers processed the carcasses on the beach (Scofield 1954:105) and possibly in the large structure mapped to the west of the station. Sengteller's notes indicate that structures mapped on the point south of Whaler's Station were the houses of the company. These may have been removed and reassembled on the island a few years later, as the houses are not present on USCS maps after 1877. The point was near the marine source of the tsunami of November 1878. The operations were moved to nearby Whaler Island in the late 1870s. The USCS also documented the whaling station that was established at Whaler's Island near Crescent City in 1855 (Chase 1869b).

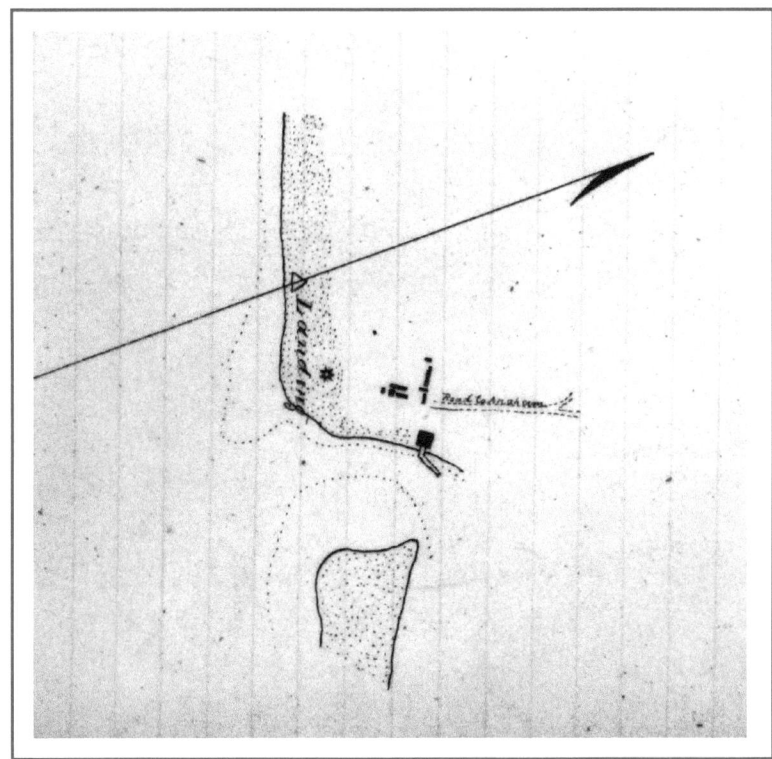

Figure 27 Field notebook map of Anaheim Landing Station (Chase 1873) showing the wharf and warehouse, nearby buildings, the lighthouse (in red) near the survey station, and the road to Anaheim. The Pacific Ocean is at the left. (Photographed by author at NARA II.)

Anaheim Landing was mapped by Chase in 1871 (Figure 27). Later known as Seal Beach, the landing included buildings, a wharf, and a lighthouse. In the year 1874 the Anaheim Landing Company exports were dominated by barley, rye, corn, beans, and wool (Los Angeles Herald 1875). But harbor improvements failed to meet demands, and by 1878 it was no longer an operating port. The port was typical of many mapped by the USCS on the California coast, supplying inland communities with imported goods while allowing exports.

The surveyors mapped several landings along the shores of the Channel Islands. Many of these show corrals nearby, indicative of the extensive ranching conducted on these islands (Livingston 2004). The surveyors considered some of these corrals to be old at the time of their initial surveys from 1853–1860, indicating that the ranching predated the US presence on Santa Cruz, Santa Rosa, and other islands. Greenwell (1856–1857) established a triangulation baseline through the Castillero sheep ranch compound on Santa Cruz Island in 1856, detailing the ranch layout at that time. One of the earliest colonial-era houses on the Channel Islands was evidently on Anacapa. Surveyor William Greenwell (1855–1860:56) described "the remains of an old house" here during his visit in 1855. The house was located near a landing on the north shore of Middle Island, which appears on the 1856 hydrographic chart without the structure shown. Recent research by Smithsonian archaeologist Torben Rick (2011) indicates that Chumash people continued to reside on this part of Anacapa during the first half of the nineteenth century, thus it is possible this residence was of Native American origin.

The USCS mapped the Russian-American Company's Fort Ross during the period when it was used as a ranch and lumber port (Figure 23), and they also mapped Port Rumiantsev at Campbell Cove on Bodega Head, at the entrance to Bodega Bay (Figure 7). The latter site included the first Russian structures built in California, possibly dating to 1809. Compared with Fort Ross, this landing was in a more protected location, and it was used extensively for shipping until the Russians closed Fort Ross in 1841 (Lightfoot 2005:124). Contemporary accounts (e.g., Lyman 1851) noted the dilapidated structures or warehouse buildings of the Russian port in the 1850s. The USCS surveyors mapped the Russian buildings in 1856 and did a more detailed rendering with topography in 1862. The map shown in Figure 7 is a portion of an 1863 tracing of the topography and other features of Bodega Head, showing the port buildings without the vegetation cover that typically appears on USCS T-sheets. The rendering appears to be detailed enough to accurately determine the location of the buildings for archaeological study and site preservation, though the site may have been destroyed or capped by fill during initial shaft excavation for a proposed Pacific Gas and Electric nuclear plant in 1961.

Early Industrial Sites

Numerous USCS field maps depict urban areas on the shores of San Francisco Bay, as industry associated with the mining-based economy was burgeoning by the early 1850s. Early maps and notes depict structures and compounds associated with shipyards, tanneries, dairies, manufacturing, canneries and smokehouses, oyster-processing plants, and warehouses. Mare Island Naval Shipyard (T-sheet no. 564, 1856) was the most extensive early

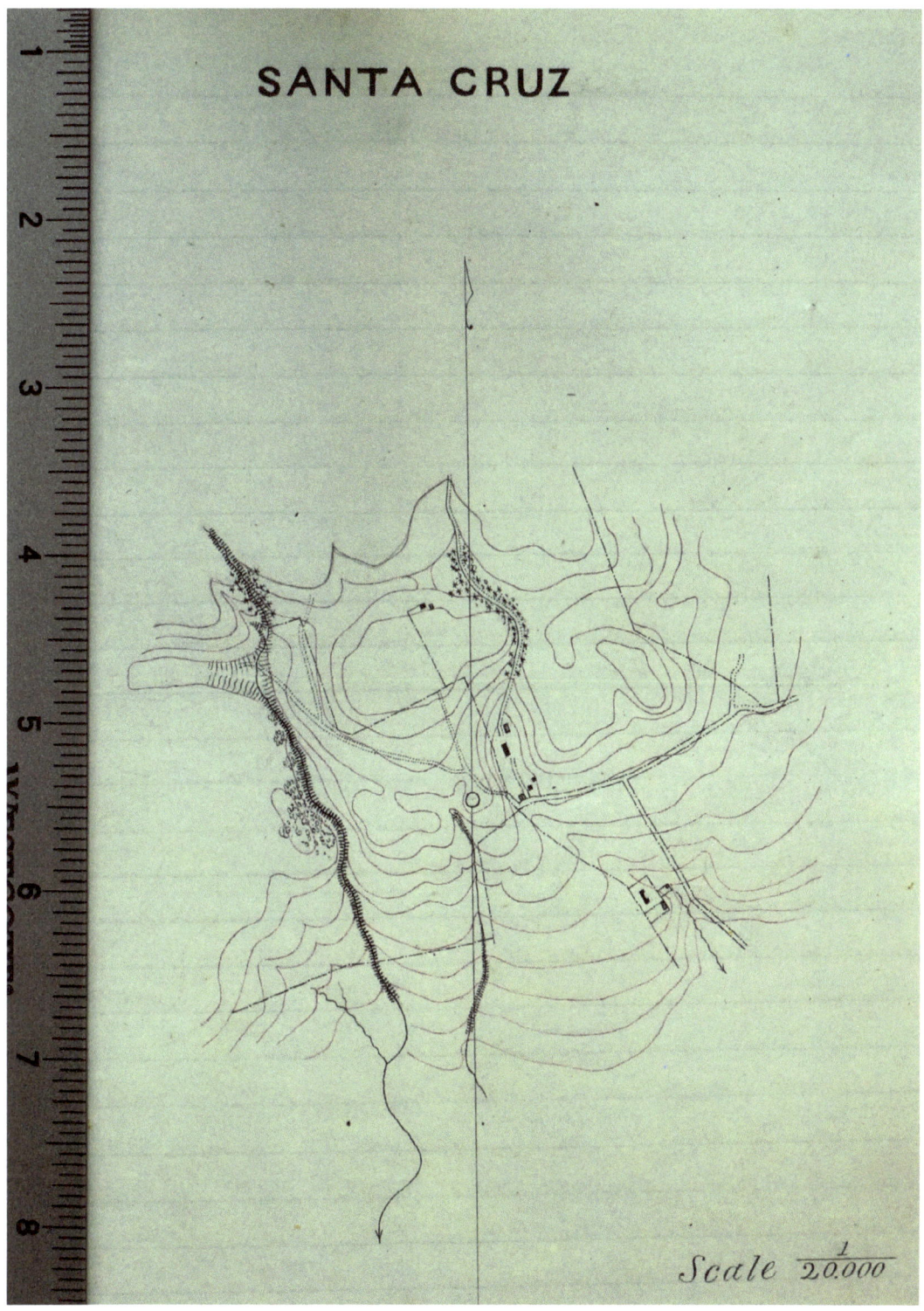

Figure 28 Pages from Cutts's (1851–1852) volume showing Santa Cruz primary triangulation station and its context, including Jordan's lime kiln (identified in the accompanying text). The rule is included in the photo to show how the scale of the map is used to determine distance: at a 1:20,000 scale, 1 in. equals 508 m. (Photographed by author at NARA II.)

industrial complex the USCS mapped in California. The agency previously played a key role in identifying a suitable location for this West Coast shipyard in 1850 (T-sheet no. 516; NOAA 2011c).

Outside the Bay Area, mapped industrial sites include quarries, lime kilns, and numerous lumber mills, some that had already been abandoned by the time the USCS completed the initial maps. In the early 1850s, Richard Cutts (1851–1852) produced a detailed map at 1:20,000 scale showing the first commercial lime kiln in Santa Cruz, which Cutts identified as "Jordan's lime kiln," located 70 m northwest of Santa Cruz primary triangulation station (Figure 28). The map also shows nearby farms and the roads connecting the kiln to the Santa Cruz embarcadero. Later lime production buildings at this site, known as the Cowell Lime Works, are still preserved on the campus of UC Santa Cruz, and were listed on the National Register in 2007 (Perry et al. 2007).

On the early federal maps of the southern California coast, industrial development is not widely depicted. This reflects the low population and largely agrarian nature of most settlement in the coastal region at the time. One exception is the Pacific Salt Works (Figure 29) at what is now Redondo Beach (Duncan-Abrams and Milkovich 1995; McLeod 2009). Prior to railroad development in the region, this large salt pond was a key source for salt mining, processing, and distribution to Los Angeles and other towns in the region. The commercial operation was established in December 1854 and mapped one year later by William Greenwell (1855–1860). The site is now California Historical Landmark no. 373. Farther south in Baja California, the USCS mapped the facilities of the *orchilla* (purple dye) processing and whaling station at Magdalena Bay (Figure 30) in 1878. Another south coast industry was hide processing. Richard Cutts (T-sheet no. 333) mapped several such buildings at La Playa, but his field notes from this survey were apparently lost (Davidson 1871). However, surveyor James Lawson (ca. 1880) had visited the area in 1850 and described La Playa in some detail:

> Lining the beach, and near high water mark, were several large buildings formerly used for storing the hides collected by the old "hide-droghers" in their trading with the Rancheros, and there stored until a sufficient quantity was obtained to load a vessel when they were shipped East.

Late nineteenth-century USCGS maps depict an even wider variety of industrial facilities, from fuel oil depots to soap factories. Some, such as those of Rodgers (1894–1896) (e.g., Figure 31) of San Francisco Bay are comparable to Sanborn Insurance Company maps in some ways.

Shipwrecks and Related Sites

Because shipwrecks presented hazards to navigation, they were normally mapped by the USCS and shown on published navigational charts. Examples include the wreck of the Pacific Mail Steamship Company's steamer *Northerner* near Centerville in Humboldt County, and the wreck of the *Winfield Scott* at Anacapa Island. In the vicinity of San Francisco Bay the large scale of early US-period shipping resulted in numerous wrecks. Assistant Augustus F. Rodgers

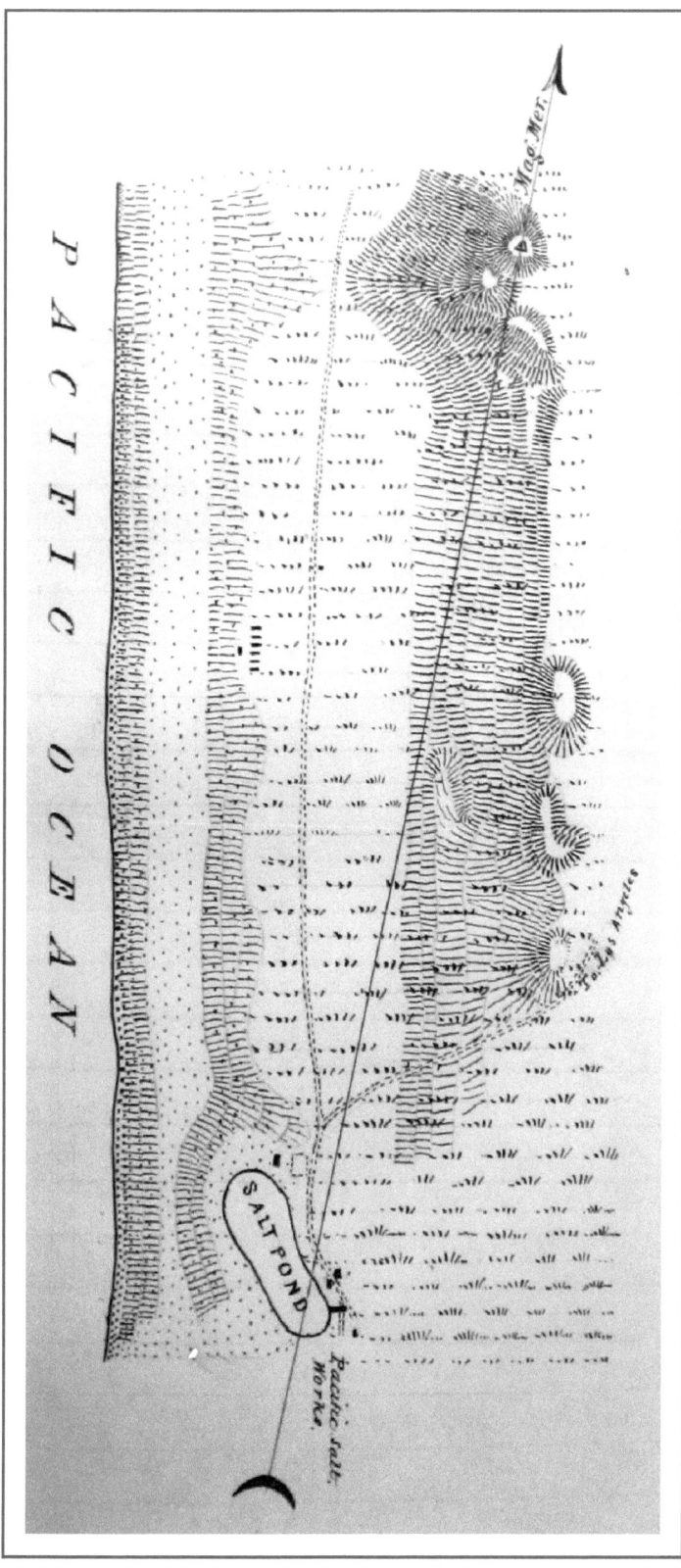

Figure 29   January 1856 map from Greenwell's (1853–1856) field notebook of the Pacific Salt Works (Engva village until 1854) at what is now part of Hermosa Beach and Redondo Beach, showing the salt pond and trails leading north and east; structures near center left of the image are not explained.   (Photographed by author at NARA II.)

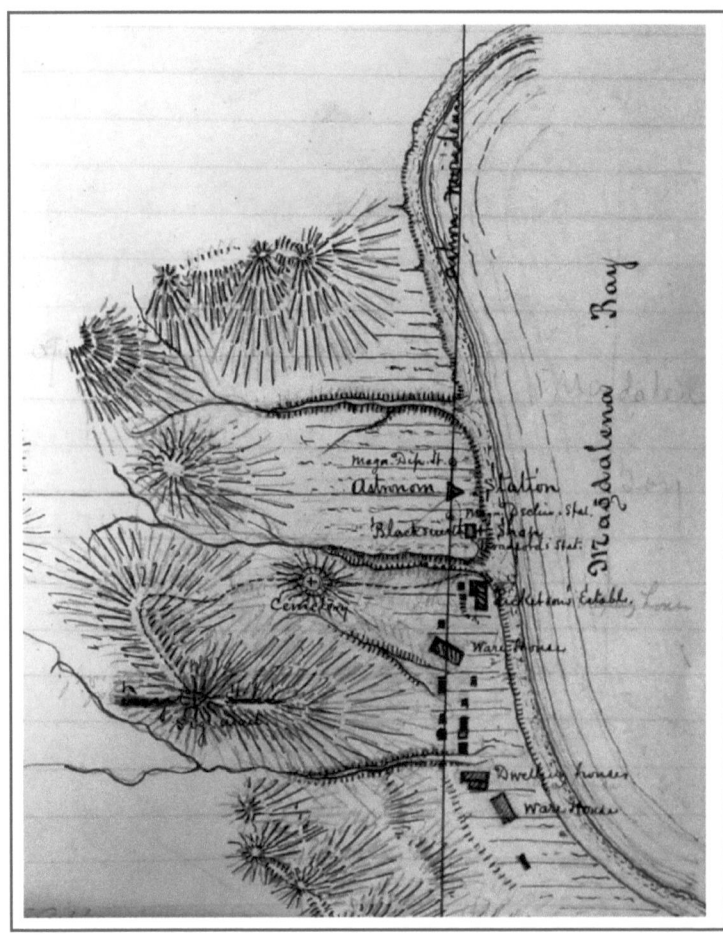

Figure 30 1878 map of the mid-nineteenth-century whaling center and *orchilla* dye processing station at Magdalena Bay, Baja California, Mexico. (USCGS field notebook no. 13089; photographed by author at NARA II.)

(1873) made a chart showing over 70 of these extending from Bodega Bay in the north to Point Pinos in the south and San Pablo Bay in the interior. This chart appears on NOAA's photo archive website. Many of the wrecks that could have been navigation hazards were described in various editions of George Davidson's *Coast Pilot*.

Over time, many of the Gold Rush–era shipwrecks deteriorated, and others were removed or became buried. The condition of many sites is unknown. Coast Survey maps and field notes are invaluable to maritime archaeologists interested in relocating these wrecks and understanding the changes they have undergone along with their settings.

One such wreck mapped by the USCGS was the USS *Edith*, a US Navy three-mast barque with an early steam engine. According to the National Park Service (2006:C-91), the *Edith* is "the oldest-known steamer and naval vessel to be lost on the west coast of America" and the wreck site may hold "the only known Ericsson-designed telescoping propeller shaft." There is compelling evidence that the *Edith* is one of the ships depicted on the California state seal (Ruhge 2001). On August 24, 1849, while en route to San Diego to transport members of the state's Constitutional Convention to Monterey, the barque wrecked on the northern Santa Barbara County coast in a dense fog at high tide. All on board survived, and the cargo and rigging were salvaged. The *Edith* became buried in the beach sand and remained so for decades. At times between 1876 and 1884 the wreck was exposed, revealing much that would be of interest to today's maritime archaeologists. This was a period of extreme drought followed by heavy rainfall (Perroy et al. 2012:1233), likely factoring in the temporary exposure of the vessel remains. An 1876 report indicates the boiler, machinery, anchors, brass ten-pounders, and piles of cannonballs were exposed during extreme low tide (Ruhge 2001). Surveyors William Greenwell (1878) and Paul Schumacher of the USCGS mapped the wreck's location in 1878 near the mouth of San Antonio Creek, on what is now Vandenberg Air Force Base (Figure 32). At the time, the wreck was well exposed and relevant as a visual reference point for relocating San Antonio Station approximately 500 m to the east in the chaparral-covered sand hills. George Davidson (1889:104–105) noted that the wreck was exposed in 1884 when "torrents from the creek washed away the sand." There are no known accounts of it being exposed again after 1884, and agricultural, residential, and military base development of the San Antonio watershed may have reduced the intensity of creek flooding over the last century. By utilizing the USCGS manuscript map of the wreck and published survey station coordinates (Baldwin 1904:590–592), accurate geophysical survey of the wreck site could determine whether the remains of the vessel are present beneath the beach sand near San Antonio Creek.

In some cases archaeological traces of wrecked vessels are represented by pieces of the ship brought up onto land during salvage operations. USCS Assistant James Lawson (1861) described such a site, the remains of a camp associated with the wreck of the US transport schooner *Captain Lincoln*, which was beached in 1852 on the southern Oregon coast. Chapter 5 presents the historical and archaeological methods my colleagues and I used in 2011–2012 to locate and study this ephemeral shipwreck camp in its coastal dune setting.

USCS records also help to clarify Gold Rush–era shipwreck history at Tomales Bay in Marin County, northwest of San Francisco. Here the USCS mapped the wreck of the *Oxford* and a structure evidently related to the wreck that may have been associated with archaeological site CA-MRN-201, investigated by multiple archaeologists (see Stewart and Praetzellis 2003:98).

The 750-ton ship *Oxford* appears to have wrecked on a reef near Tomales Point on July 12, 1852 (Daily Alta California 1852). Although the 1854 T-sheet (no. 439) of Tomales Bay shows the wreck of the *Oxford* within the bay on a sand flat north of Tom's Point, 1852 newspaper accounts of the wreck and Rodgers's (1873) regional shipwreck map indicate the *Oxford* initially came to rest near Tomales Point. A volume on Marin County history by Munro-Fraser suggests the wreck near Tom's Point, within Tomales Bay, may have been a different ship. According to Munro-Fraser (1880:124), the well-known local resident Thomas Wood, also known as Tom Vaquero, observed the wreck of the *Cambridge* in 1849, in roughly the location where the USCS mapped the *Oxford* on the 1861 preliminary chart and the 1854 T-sheet. While it is possible that two ships with different names associated with leading British universities wrecked at Tomales Bay during the Gold Rush, it seems more

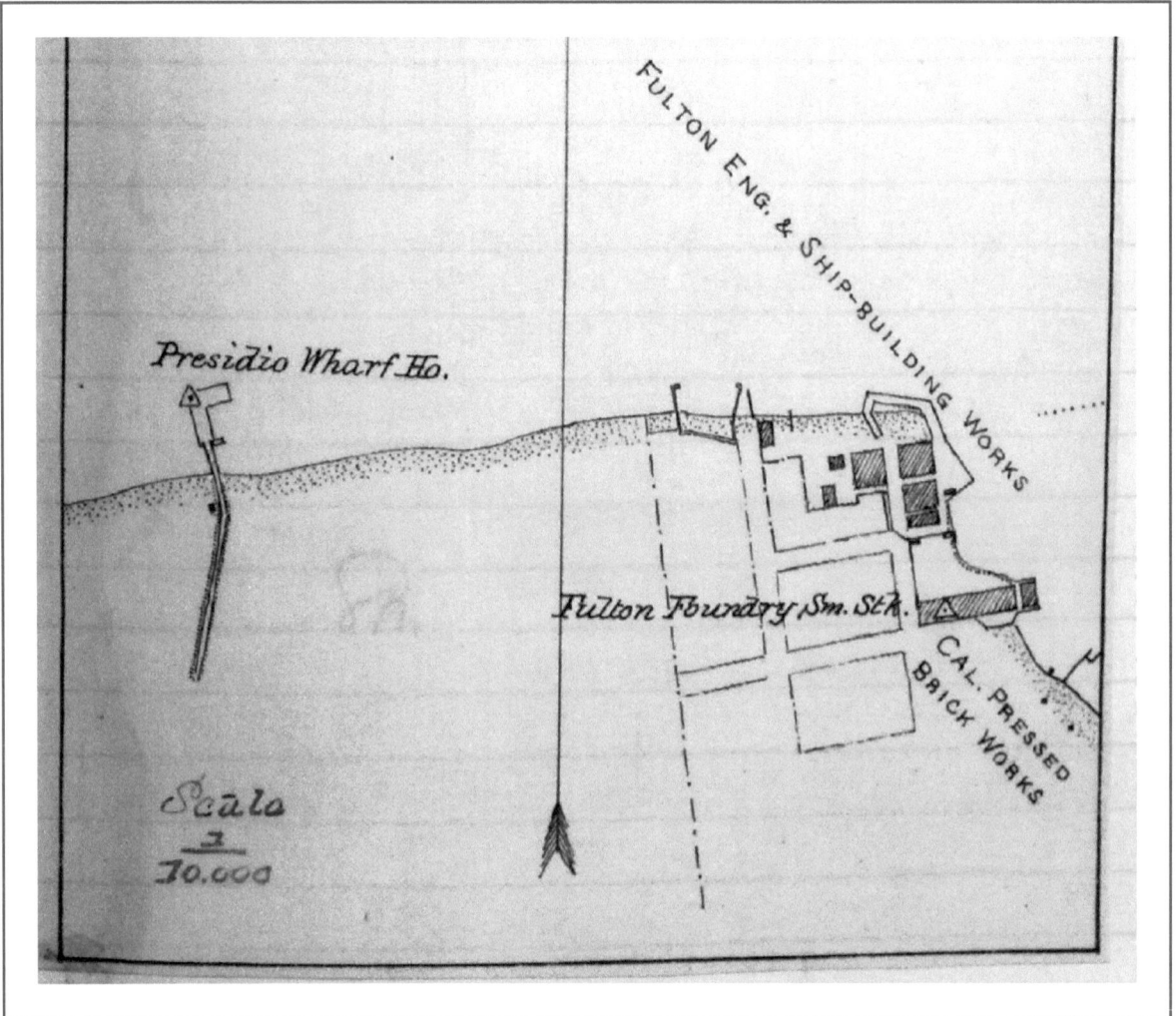

Figure 31 Rodgers's (1894–1896) map of the Presidio Wharf House Station and Fulton Foundry Smoke Stack Station on the north shore of San Francisco. (Photographed by author at NARA II.)

likely that Munro-Fraser recalled the wrong name and date some 15 years after he was told about the wreck. The wreck became locally well known because Thomas Wood salvaged the ship's cabin to use as his home on the nearby shore (Collier and Thalman 1996; Munro-Fraser 1880:124). George A. Fairfield (1855–1858) of the USCS mapped a survey position at Tom's Point on June 7, 1856, and referenced the station as "immediately above, and to the Southward of Tom Vaquero's house." This house is the only structure that appears on Fairfield's notebook map, which may be the only one ever made of this unusual structure fashioned from a shipwreck.

There are other instances of the USCS mapping beached vessels that may or may not have later been dismantled, such as a schooner grounded in 1871 at Sand Beach Station near Bolsas Creek (Chase 1872). Ships that were entirely salvaged or were completely buried were often left off of subsequent USCS topographic maps and hydrographic charts.

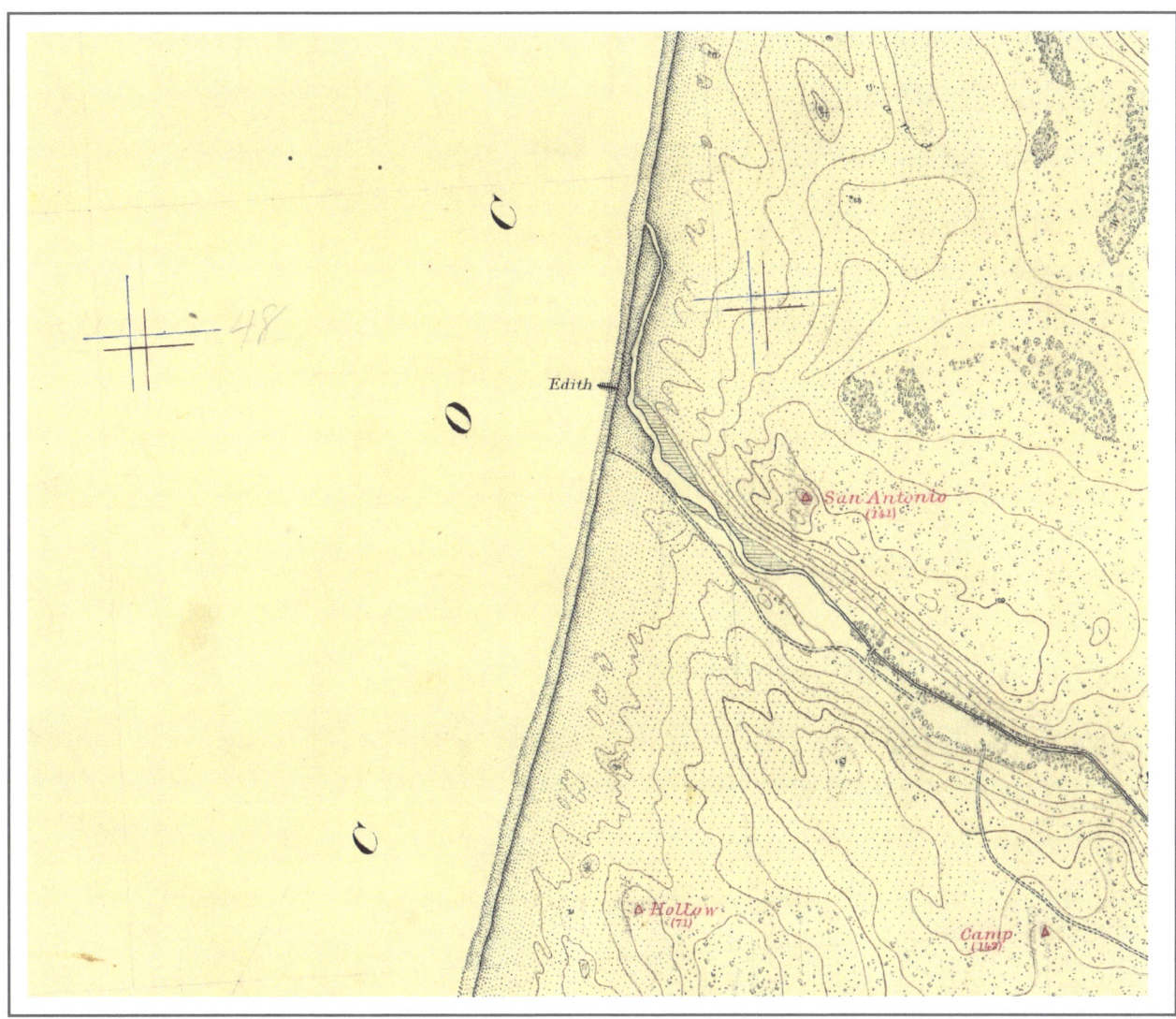

Figure 32   Portion of 1879 T-sheet no. 1855b showing the location of the USS *Edith* wreck site at the mouth of San Antonio Creek and three of Greenwell's (1878) mapping stations. Geographic coordinates for these stations were tabulated by Baldwin (1904) in a USCGS annual report. Using these station coordinates to register the image as a GIS layer, the geographic coordinates for the *Edith* in 1878 can be determined with some precision. (Scanned by John Cloud at NARA II.)

Fortifications

Beginning in the early 1850s, the USCS assisted an army and navy commission tasked with assessing sites for Pacific coast forts and military bases and locations for lighthouses (Cutts 1853a; Theberge 2011:354). Their work involved assessing existing presidios and forts, as well as determining locations for new defensive facilities, navigational buoys, and lighthouses. Fortifications were also prominent references for maps of nearby stations, and in some cases survey stations were set within the grounds of a fort, such as Drum Barracks in Los Angeles (Chase 1872:7).

The USCS mapped individual buildings at several forts, including Fort Humboldt (T-sheet no. 474, 1854), Fort Bragg (T-sheet no. 1363b, 1873), Fort Point and Presidio San Francisco (Cutts 1851–1852), Presidio San Diego (T-sheet no. 333, 1851), Fort Mervine and El Castillo battery (T-sheet no. 357, 1851–1852), Department of the Pacific headquarters in Benicia (Hydrographic Sheet no. 5686, 1869), and the government barracks on Catalina Island (T-sheet no. 1603, 1873). Only a few structures associated with Russian Fort Ross appear on the 1878 Sengteller map (Figure 23) that shows the fort in the Call Ranch period, but two of the fort's circular blockhouses are still present. On smaller-scale USCS field sketches the plotted locations of Fort Terwah and Fort Gaston appear, and these maps provide other useful context such as trails (Davidson 1860). Locations that later became military installations were also mapped in detail, such as Angel Island in San Francisco Bay in 1852 (Cutts 1851–1852).

Some USCS Descriptions of Stations notebooks depict areas surveyed for lighthouse reservations, such as Point Arena in 1880 (Sengteller 1870). Cartographic sketch maps and T-sheets depict several early lighthouse locations such as Point Hueneme in 1857 and Point Pinos in 1851. However, field notes generated for the army and navy commission may be archived separately from other Descriptions of Stations notebooks. Sengteller's (1870) volume is the only one I have encountered in the GA Series that is specific to a lighthouse reservation area.

Among the early USCS maps were depictions of presidios and related structures. The ruins of El Castillo battery were mapped and labeled on an 1852 T-sheet (no. 357 of Monterey Bay, Figure 33). San Diego Presidio was depicted on the 1851 T-sheet (no. 333) of the bay. A sketch and map by William McMurtrie shows the adobe walls of the compound (Trent and Seymour 2010:106). The USCS set no survey markers in the immediate vicinity of the presidio, and in any event field notes from the 1851 survey were lost, so there is no description of a station or small area map at this location. Yet the topographic sheet plane table map was used to guide museum research and archaeological interpretations of the site until an 1820 map was identified at the Bancroft Library in 1984 (Bartel 1991; MacMullen 1962).

Cutts's (1851–1852) sketch of Presidio San Francisco (Figure 8) was drawn to locate the survey station on the hill to the west, but along with the accompanying station map, the rendering is of great value in the interpretation of the site's history during the Gold Rush. The sketch was likely drawn in 1851 (Bache 1852:86, 442). Cutts's drawing is in marked contrast to the well-known engravings done for publications of this period. Whereas the widely presented Soule (1855:263) engraving shows prominent mountains in the background, troops in formation, and vaqueros on horseback, Cutts depicted a treeless landscape, less prominent structures, and a flagpole, in addition to the hilltop survey marker. A faint fence line surrounds the compound, but there is no sense that this was a defensible walled compound. It is also very different from the 1843 Scattergood engraving (National Park Service 2012), which shows the structures in a waterfront setting along with conifer trees lining drainages. The buildings do not appear to be oriented along a rectangular perimeter in this earlier rendering.

That Cutts took the time to include this sketch suggests that he may have intended to memorialize the Presidio as he had the remains of Lewis and Clark's Fort Clatsop at the mouth

Figure 33 Fort Mervine and the ruins of El Castillo battery in Monterey on T-sheet no. 357 (Cutts 1851–1852). (NARA II scan courtesy of NOAA Central Library.)

of the Columbia that same year (Byram 2005). Yet Cutts's sketch clearly does not glorify the Presidio. It may be the most representative image for this period, though it lacks entirely the depiction of people and their activities. The accompanying map in the 1851–1852 notebook shows the layout of the structures in plan, and it is likely an accurate representation of their size and relative position. Cutts's map shows fewer structures than maps used by the National Park Service and other researchers investigating the history and archaeology of the Presidio (e.g., Wolfram 2010:15). The Presidio Hill Station map and drawing will allow more resolution of the architectural nadir of the adobe compound, a key issue in the archaeological study of the Presidio (Praetzellis et al. 2008:13).

Ranchos and Adobes

The USCS records are among several categories of maps that depict ranchos and other dwelling sites associated with important individuals from the early US period in California. They provide precise mapping of some structures, and they often include contextual details relevant to archaeological studies.

In recent years there has been interest among archaeologists and historians in the early adobes associated with Rancho Boca de Santa Monica (Goodman 2009; Marquez 2011). Specifically, the Ysidro Reyes adobe and the Francisco Marquez adobe are recognized as important historical places, though only the latter has received landmark status. The Marquez adobe is thought to have been within the Marquez-Reyes cemetery, San Lorenzo Garden (Historic-Cultural Monument 685). Both adobes were built in the 1840s, and they were mapped in 1853 by William Greenwell (1855–1860) when he surveyed the shore of Santa Monica Bay, which he knew as Bahía Ona (Davidson 1887:196).

Field notes accompany Greenwell's 1856 map of Santa Monica Station, which shows a road and two structures (Figure 19). The one on the left in the canyon was likely the Marquez adobe, and a later USCS map confirms the one on the rim to the right was the Reyes adobe. Chase's (1875) notes and map of the same locality identify the ruins of the Cedro Reyes adobe (Figure 18). The ruins were probably labeled for consistency, as surveyors often tried to refer to previously identified landmarks in revisiting a position. Chase was not able to relocate the station; the small scale and lack of map ratio on the earlier map likely are reasons.

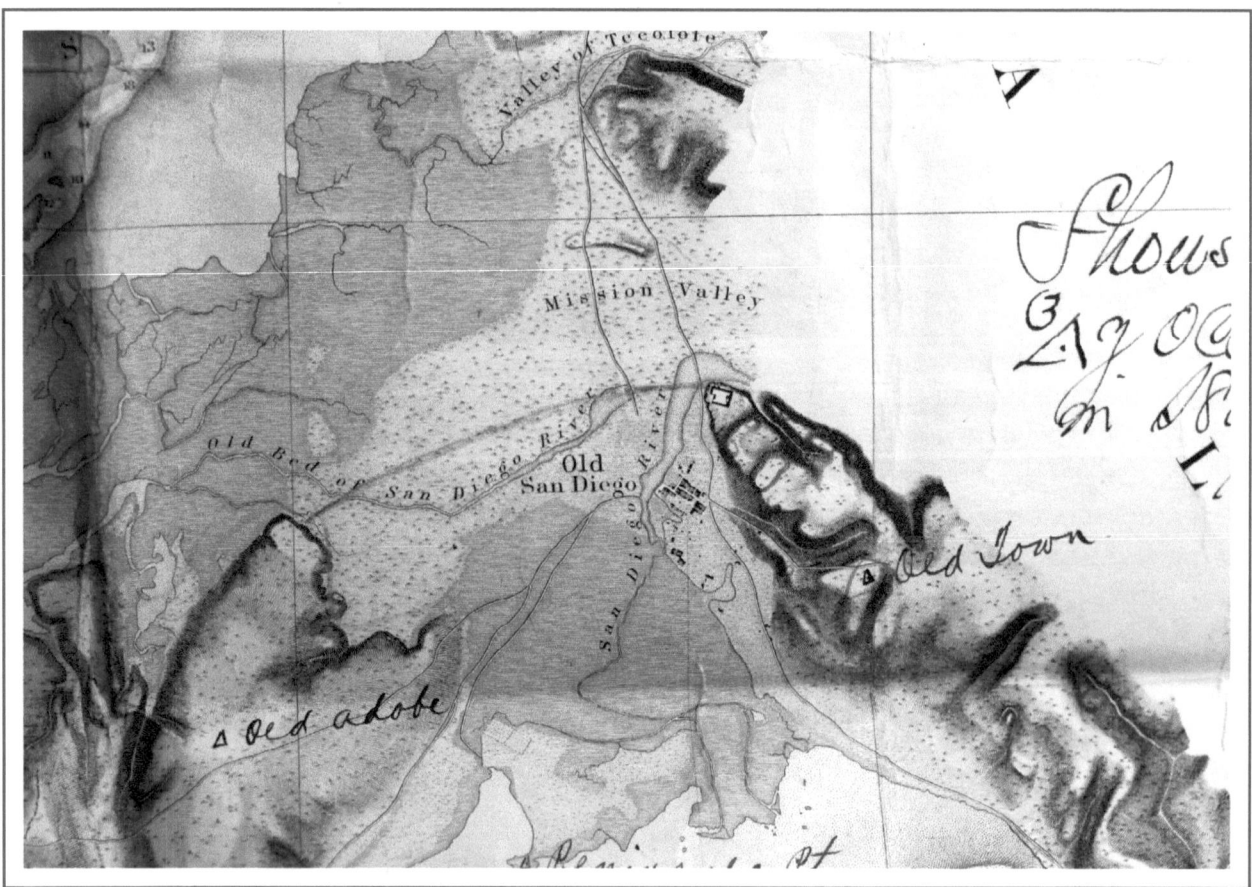

Figure 34 Old Adobe and Old Town stations plotted by Rodgers in 1887 on a portion of a published 1859 T-sheet (no. 606) of north San Diego Bay that also shows town buildings and the presidio. (Photographed by author at NARA II.)

Both structures were destroyed in the early twentieth century, so the USCS maps are relevant to the landmark status and context of both adobe sites. These structures also appear on T-sheet no. 1427, but they are not labeled. Other features on the Chase map of Santa Monica Canyon show the rapid development of this setting between 1856 and 1875.

Augustus F. Rodgers's 1887 depiction of an adobe ruin (Figure 34) on the northeastern portion of the Point Loma uplands at San Diego Bay is detailed, and as the survey station was within the ruins, the locational information is particularly precise. Baldwin (1904:544) gives the geographic coordinates of the position. Rodgers (1887b) recorded the dimensions of the "old adobe" as 10 x 15 ft. and described it as the ruins of a house. He noted that it was the only house of its kind on the hill between San Diego Bay to the south and False Bay to the north. This would have been uphill and northeast of La Playa, mapped by Richard Cutts's survey party in 1851 (T-sheet no. 333). The condition of the adobe as a ruin in 1887 does not clarify its antiquity, but this may be the ruin of one of the early residences of the mission or secularization era. Although the structure does not appear on the Cutts map or the printed 1859 map that Rodgers used as a plane table sheet, on both maps a road leads toward the Old Adobe area from Old Town. The 1851 T-sheet shows part of this road but does not cover the area of the adobe. Archaeological testing or land record comparisons may further elucidate the structure's origin.

The Richardson Rancho in Sausalito was the third residence of Captain William Richardson, the well-known ranchero and port supervisor who traveled to San Francisco Bay on a whaling vessel in 1822 shortly after Mexican independence, and later married the daughter of the commandant at the Presidio. For many years he served as port captain, and in Sausalito he managed a water source for ships taking on supplies in San Francisco Bay. Richardson was an associate of several Native Americans in the area, and Native people reportedly worked on his ranch and in Sausalito-based shipping operations such as piloting (Goerke 2007:162–163). There are indications that his ranch buildings were located on a traditional village site (CA-MRN-3; Nelson 1907), and the Native people with whom he collaborated in business and farming may have had ties to this village.

Although the T-sheets and hydrographic charts typically do not record the names of the owners of mapped dwellings and rancho compounds, the associated field notes often provide these details. T-sheet no. 1396 (Figure 5) shows mid-nineteenth-century ranch buildings and related linear features on Santa Rosa Island. Among several other California ranchos mapped in varying detail are Rancho Dos Pueblos near Santa Barbara (Greenwell 1862–1863), Centinela Rancho in Westminster near Inglewood (Chase 1875), and the Castillero Rancho on Santa Cruz Island (Greenwell 1856–1857). The estates of Agostin Haraszthy, the vineyard specialist, and Carey Jones, the land claims attorney, on the San Francisco Peninsula were depicted by Cutts (1851–1852). The Call Ranch at Fort Ross is an example of the many north coast ranches and farms mapped by the USCS in the 1870s.

The USCS mapped and described a ranch in the hills east of Concord (Eimbeck 1876) that was one of the earliest African American ranches in the Bay Area (Figure 35). Milford and Mary Jane Lowry moved from New York to homestead there in the 1860s or early 1870s, receiving their land patent in 1876. On occasion, Lowry grain and beef may have been shipped

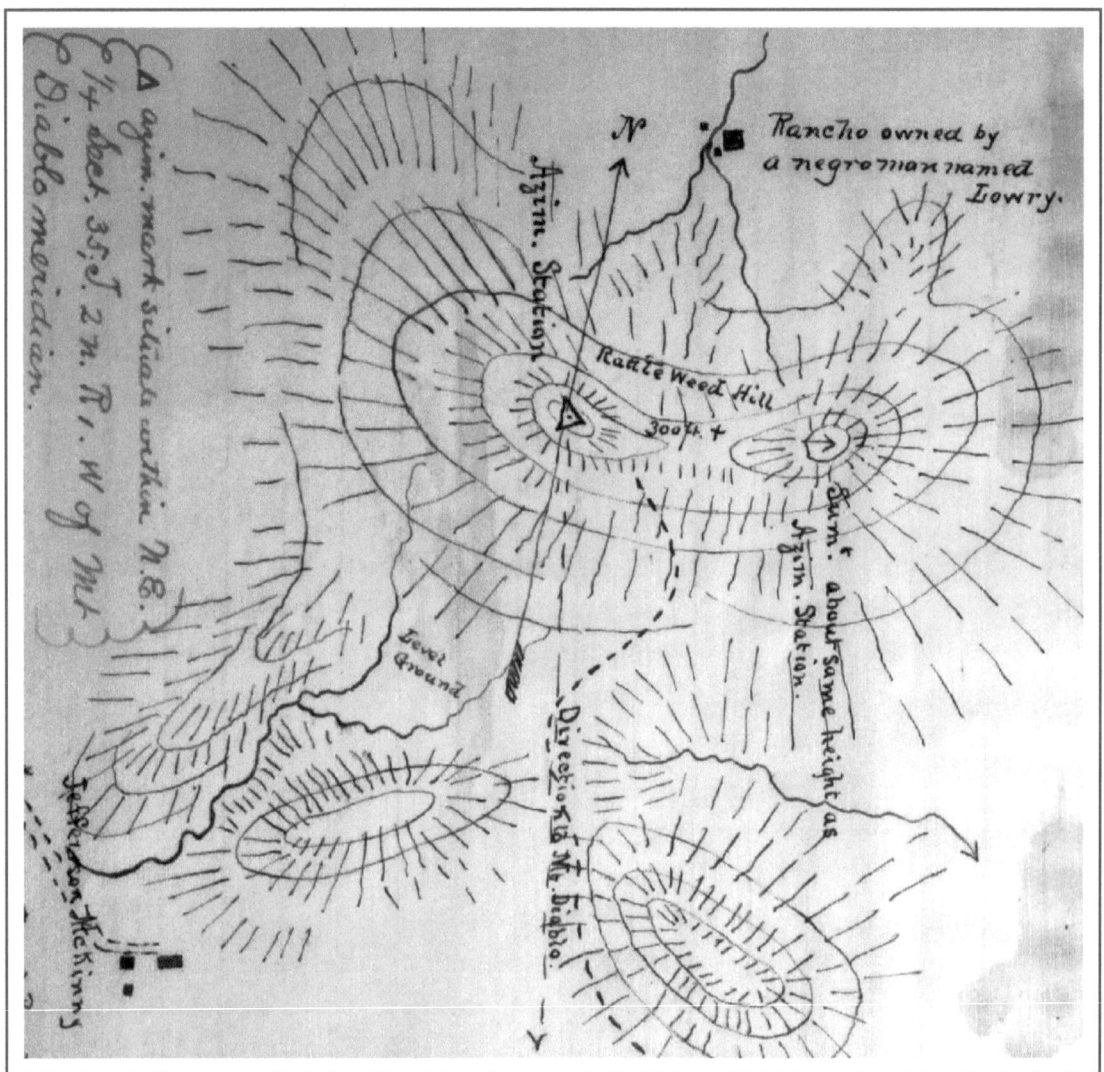

Figure 35 Detail from Eimbeck's (1876) field notebook, Mt. Diablo Azimuth section, showing the Lowry Ranch in eastern Contra Costa County. (Photographed by author at NARA II.)

through nearby Seal Bluff Landing, adding an early dimension to African American history at Port Chicago Naval Magazine National Memorial. It is not clear if this family continued to ranch there after the 1880s, but the compound appeared on USGS maps and aerial photos into the 1990s.

In 2011, I submitted a California Historical Resources Information System primary record for this property to the Northwest Information Center at Sonoma State University based on the archival research. Records at this office indicate that the area had been surveyed archaeologically prior to its development as a landfill in the 1990s, but no archaeological site was recorded in the vicinity of the Lowry Ranch.

The Henderson Ranch site (35-CS-221) at Coos Bay, Oregon, was documented archaeologically as part of a Section 106 project (Byram 2006). Related archival research demonstrated that it had been among a group of ranches used as refuges for Native Americans escaping starvation and disease at the Coast Reservation in the 1860s. The land claimant,

John Henderson, was one of several US settlers who had close ties to the Coos Bay Indians, and stored their canoes when they fled parties of soldiers from the reservation agency. The archaeological materials at the site can shed light on this important period in Native American history on the southern Oregon coast. James Lawson (1861) of the USCS and E. F. Dickens (1889) of the USCGS mapped the ranch and surrounding area, and these maps will guide archaeologists conducting further investigations of the site's history.

The two-story frame house of California's first US-period governor, Peter H. Burnett, was mapped by the USCS in Alviso, before the structure was moved to San Jose in 1854. A photograph of the building is in the archives of the San Jose Public Library (2011). Its high facade suggests that Burnett had expected a town to arise in the vicinity of his home, but only one other structure is present near his house on the Cutts (1851–1852) map.

Summary tables in this chapter present colonial site information such as trinomials and NRHP resource designations, geographic location, site type, and USCS records used as sources. Table 1 includes archaeologically recorded sites that were documented in part by the USCS. Table 2 presents sites that were described as ruins or archaeological deposits by USCS surveyors but lack modern archaeological records. Table 3 includes locations where significant archaeological deposits may be present based on observations recorded by the USCS.

These are only a few examples of the thousands of colonial sites mapped in USCS records and the hundreds of these described in varying detail in field notebooks and reports. Historical archaeological projects will benefit immensely from the use of these documents as they become available to researchers.

Table 1 Archaeologically recorded Colonial sites updated with USCS records.

Trinomial or National Register Type	Name	County	Site Type	Primary Records	Archaeological Information
AB-22 (temporary no.)	Chino, San Nicolas Island	Ventura	historic scatter, camp	Forney (1879)	minimum age of camp, well
CA-CCO-506h	Chinese Fishing Village	Contra Costa	buildings, wharves, fences	T-sheet no. 2445 (1898)	structures, sectional community layout
National Landmark	Fort Ross	Sonoma	fortification, ranch, landing	Sengteller (1876–1879)	structures, linear features, and landscape
CA-MRN-201 vicinity	Tom Vaquero house	Marin	residence, trade center	Fairfield (1855–1858)	location, orientation of house
National Landmark	El Presidio Real de San Francisco	San Francisco	fortification, adobes	Cutts (1851–1852); T-sheet no. 314 (1851)	architecture of adobes in 1851, setting, outlying buildings
NRHP District	Fort Mervine	Monterey	fortification	T-sheet no. 357 (1852)	layout of buildings within earthworks; town and setting
CA Landmark 309	Mission Santa Barbara	Santa Barbara	fortification, village	Harrison (1853); T-sheet no. 373 (1852)	sequence of reconstruction
CA-SDI-38	Presidio San Diego	San Diego	fortification	T-sheet no. 333 (1851)	fortification layout
NRHP 07001220	Jordan's lime kiln	Santa Cruz	lime kiln, residences	Cutts (1851–1852)	Jordan's lime kiln and its setting
35-CS-221	Henderson Ranch	Coos (OR)	historic scatter	Dickens (1889)	dwellings associated with Native American refuge
National Memorial	Seal Bluff	Contra Costa	landing, buildings	Greenwell (1866)	Seal Bluff Landing warehouses and wharf
NRHP Ranching District	Santa Rosa Island Ranchos	Santa Barbara	rancho	Forney (1872); T-sheet no. 1326 (1872)	ranch buildings and other facilities
35-CS-277	Camp Castaway	Coos (OR)	military camp, shipwreck	Lawson (1861); T-sheet no. 846 (1861), Wreck Station	location and description of lodge, shipwreck parts, dune setting

Table 2 Colonial sites recognized by USCS surveyors as archaeological or in ruins.

Trinomial or National Register Type	Name	County	Site Type	Primary Records	Archaeological Information
no site record	Old Adobe	San Diego	adobe walls (residence?)	Rodgers (1887b)	dimensions and location of outlying adobe ruin
NRHP District	El Castillo	Monterey	fortifications	T-sheet no. 357 (1852)	ruins of Mexican battery
no site record	Port Rumiantsev	Marin	buildings	Fairfield (1855–1858); T-sheet no. 883 (1862)	location and outline of three Russian-era buildings, corrals, landing
no site record	Anacapa Island house	Ventura	ruined house	Greenwell (1855–1860)	location of "old" residence in 1855, possibly Chumash
no site record	Ysidro Reyes Adobe	Los Angeles	ruined house	Chase (1875); Greenwell (1855–1860)	location and layout of adobe house; names of former owner
no site record	USS *Edith* wreck	Santa Barbara	shipwreck	Greenwell (1878); T-sheet no. 1555b (1879)	location of shipwreck while it was exposed in beach sand
NRHP no. 173 CA	SS *Northerner* wreck	Humboldt	shipwreck and memorial	Rodgers (1869, 1872); T-sheet no. 1135 (1869)	changing location of cross; location of metal wreck components

Table 3 Colonial sites documented by the USCS with no confirmed archaeological remains.

Trinomial or National Register Type	Name	County	Site Type	Primary Records	Archaeological Information
no site record	Lowry Ranch	Contra Costa	ranch buildings	Eimbeck (1876)	African American–owned ranch in Contra Costa County ca. 1860s
NRHP 91001093	Whaler Station	San Luis Obispo	cabins	Sengteller (1871)	locations of original whaler station buildings before island used.
CA-MRN-3 vicinity	Richardson Rancho	Marin	ranch buildings	Cutts (1851–1852)	locations and outlines of adobes and outlying buildings
no site record	Burnett house	Alviso	residence	Cutts (1851–1852)	location and context of first US-period CA governor's residence
no site record	Barry's Hotel	Alameda	commercial area	T-sheet no. 1622b (1873)	1873 public gathering area at what later became Sproul Plaza
NRHP Ranching District	Santa Cruz Island; Castillero	Santa Barbara	ranch buildings	Greenwell (1855–1860): Shaw Station	layout of ranch buildings, trails
CA Landmark 373	Pacific Salt Works	Los Angeles	salt processing, residences	Greenwell (1855–1860)	initial construction of salt processing facility, residences

Chapter 4
Maps, Notes, and Sketches in Archaeological Interpretation: Native American Sites

Native American sites represented in USCS records from California are primarily residential, consisting of villages, mounds, and caves, though the latter two site types may not have been used for habitation in some cases. Trail sites were also mapped. The countless other types of Native American sites that have limited or no structures present as visual markers were not typically mapped, such as fisheries, though wooden fish traps in Oregon were mapped (Rockwell 1878). While the term "village" is often associated with Native people in USCS notes, this is not always the case; the term "ranchería" was also commonly used in reference to Native peoples' dwellings in California (United States Surveyor-General of California 1876:197), though the term was less common farther north on the coast. Mounds were sometimes identified as shell mounds or rancherías by USCS staff, but in other cases their presence has been determined here by relating mapped topography to later information about an archaeological site, such as Nelson's (1907) field notes. It is important to note that in the field notes, the term "mound" was also used at times to refer to noncultural topographic features.

Native American Villages

In some instances the USCS surveyors identified Native American archaeological residential sites based on the presence of stone tools, fire pits, house rings, and other cultural material. Most Native residential sites identified by the USCS were either occupied or recently abandoned village sites or archaeological mounds. Each of these groups is discussed separately.

Maps and descriptions of Native communities along the coast north of San Francisco Bay and on the south coast of California show that many Native people continued to reside in traditional residential communities through the middle and later nineteenth century. Numerous Native American village sites were mapped by the US Coast Survey, with many appearing on T-sheets and published hydrographic charts. Surveyors saw Native peoples' structures as useful landmarks. During the 1850s through 1870s, these communities were seen by surveyors as comparable to settler communities in terms of their permanence and relevance for survey maps, provided structures were present.

Native Americans had valuable knowledge of the areas surrounding mapping stations. Often there were individuals from Native villages who assisted in surveying, such as the Yurok man who undertook the dangerous 200-foot free climb to secure a rope ladder on Flint Rock, near the mouth of the Klamath River, and the others from his tribe who piloted the canoes that brought surveyors to Station Rock (Chase 1872–1873). Native Americans frequently assisted surveyors in piloting canoes or whaleboats across bars and to offshore islands, as depicted in several of James Alden's watercolors (Stenzel 1975). When Benjamin Colonna established mountaintop stations to triangulate the Coast Range in 1878, he had extensive assistance from George McLeary and other Native people at Cahto Village in Mendocino County, where Cahto Station had been established in 1860 (Colonna 1878:82). Residents of the village were heavily involved as guides, hosts, and suppliers of equipment. Native people also assisted the USCS with climbs of inland peaks such as Mt. Shasta. Colonna's (1880a) published account of this climb provides less information than his field notes (Colonna 1880b:47–53), which include the names of the Native American woman and men who provided assistance as guides and packers.

A key goal of USCS triangulation was to depict structures and other landmarks that were useful for relocating mapping positions and survey markers. While there was no systematic effort to differentiate the ethnic makeup of the communities mapped by the Coast Survey, agency staff often recorded this information as part of contextual description. Historian John Cloud (2007) has noted that the USCGS had a specific directive to record Native American place-names while mapping the coast, and many of these appear in Coast Pilot volumes and on T-sheets. In this regard the USCS differed from agencies such as the General Land Office, whose surveyors often chose to overlook Native communities as they subdivided the land for government sale.

Through the 1870s, villages were depicted and identified as "Native" or "Indian" around Humboldt Bay, Smith River, Lake Earl, the Klamath River, and Tomales Bay. Just across the Oregon border at the Chetco River, Alexander W. Chase mapped the village of Tcet-xo in 1870, demonstrating that the village was restored after US settlers killed many of the people and burned the houses there in 1853 (Douthit 2002:123). Chase's topography later appeared on a USCGS hydrographic chart (USCGS 1891). This record was important in planning a Chetco Indian memorial by Siletz tribal members of Chetco descent (Rice 2009). Recently the map of the village was used to protect the site during emergency harbor reconstruction after March 2011 tsunami damage (Byram 2011), an example of the value of Coast Survey records in West Coast cultural resource management.

In some cases, USCS manuscript maps clarify ethnographers' portrayal of village locations. On an 1854 T-sheet (no. 474), the USCS plotted the location of a Native American village that may have been part of the Wiyot community of Ikso'ri at the mouth of the Mowitch (i.e., Elk) River. Although Loud (1918:270) had referenced the published 1858 USCS chart of Humboldt Bay in discussing the sandspit on which the village was reportedly located, the village itself does not appear on this 1858 chart. Ikso'ri appears to have been one of the larger villages on the shores of Humboldt Bay, yet Loud plotted it on a narrow sandspit separating the river from the bay. He indicated that the sandspit on which Ikso'ri was located had been washed away. The 1854 T-sheet shows a village over a quarter mile to the south of the location Loud plotted for Ikso'ri, where the sandspit met the bay shoreline. This setting may have been more suited to long-term, multi-season residence than the tip of the narrow, erosive sandspit to the north, though the entire peninsula that formed the left riverbank may have been within the area associated with the village.

In contrast with the north coast, the USCS mapped fewer Native villages in central and southern California. A key factor in the difference is likely related to the role of missions in southern California (Lightfoot 2005). The multiethnic nature of some communities after mission secularization may have also meant that few were identified as "Indian." Remnants of the historic village of Engva (Woodbury 1960) may have been among the structures Greenwell (1855–1860) mapped in January 1855 at the salt pond at Redondo Beach, a year after the US relocated this community to mission villages (McLeod 2009). Former mission villages that were predominantly Native American were mapped, including the ruins of the Mission Santa Barbara village (1852 T-sheet no. 373; Harrison 1853) (Figure 36). A Luiseño ranchería near Mission San Luis Rey is simply labeled "village" on an 1851 sketch attributed to James Alden (ca. 1851) (Figure 37), though it is described in other USCS documents. Several other Native residences in southern California were mapped among the buildings of various ranchos, often associated with named rancheros in the USCS field notes.

Some north coast Native American communities were mapped but not identified as Native. For example the Coast Miwok communities at Bodega Bay and nearby Smith Creek (Lightfoot 2005:212; Schneider 2007) appear on maps beginning in the 1850s. In the 1870s the communities at Gualala and Stewart's Point were mapped (Sengteller 1876–1879), but their Native residents were not identified as such.

A great number of trails appear on USCS maps from the California coast. In some instances these locations are specified as Native American trails in other documents, such as the Old Salt Road inland from the salt pond at what is now Redondo Beach, partially mapped by Greenwell in 1856 (Figure 29), that had reportedly been in use by the Gabrielino for centuries (Kirkman 1937; McLeod 2009). Yet more often these routes were simply shown as trails, sometimes with endpoint labels. As these maps of trails are related to ethnographic discussions and other local history, it is likely that the Native origin of several trails shown in the USCS manuscript records will be clarified. A trail mapped on Santa Cruz Island passed two caves that Greenwell (1856–1857:50) recognized as holding Native American archaeological materials, including mussel shell and basketry. This precedes de Cessac's documentation of Santa Cruz Island cave sites (de Cessac 1951; Moratto 1984:123), though unlike de Cessac, Greenwell is not known to have disseminated his findings.

One residential cave site that was mapped by the USCS was used as a seasonal residence by a well-known individual on San Nicolas Island, the most remote of the Channel Islands. This is among the most important historical places identified and mapped by the US Coast Survey in the nineteenth century. The cave was associated with the Nicoleño Indian woman who resided on the island alone for 18 years, from 1835 to 1853. The story of the lone woman's experience was widely recounted in newspapers after she was brought from the island to Santa Barbara, where she died from illness seven weeks later. A fictionalized account of

Figure 36 Portion of a preliminary sketch of Santa Barbara (Harrison 1853) based on the 1852 T-sheet no. 373. The mission and the village of La Cieneguita are in the hills in the upper left, and Burton Mound is on the floodplain at the lower right near Observatory Station at the shoreline. Unlike T-sheets, this is an engraving print and was more widely reproduced. (Photographed by author at NARA II.)

her life in the 1961 novel *Island of the Blue Dolphins* made more recent generations aware of her solitary existence on the island.

Despite extensive research on the topic and historical recounting of the lone woman's "rescue" from the island, there has been no specific historical site on San Nicolas associated with this unique individual. However, navy archaeologist Steve Schwartz (2010, 2012b) has found that for a century there were occasional reports of visits to a cave that held residential debris, fiber work, and other items that were attributed to the lone woman. George Nidever and other fur hunters who stayed with the woman for a month before leaving with her for Santa Barbara claimed that the woman lived in the cave during part of the year and in open shelters at other times. Unfortunately there was no formal archaeological examination of the cave before it was lost in a landslide or buried by dune sand, probably in the 1950s.

When USCS assistant Stehman Forney and his survey team mapped several primary triangulation positions across San Nicolas Island in 1879, they mapped and described what they identified as an Indian cave where Native American artifacts were present. According to their account, this was "a large cave formerly inhabited by a wild Indian woman, who lived there alone for 18 years" (Forney 1879). They named a nearby signal Cave Station (Figures 38 and 39).

In 2012, Schwartz (2012b) reported results of archaeological investigations conducted by his office and by students led by archaeologist René Vellanoweth of California State University, Los Angeles, in the vicinity of the cave described by Forney in 1879. The location is labeled "Indian Cave" on T-sheet no. 1523 (1879), which Schwartz had scanned at the National Archives. I had provided him with photos of Forney's (1879) fieldnotes, which included distance and bearing to the cave from Cave Station, along with the observation that this cave had been the residence of the lone woman (Figure 39). The navy excavations uncovered the mouth of a large cave, and by the fall of 2012 the team had excavated the length of the cave, which was filled with dune sand. Although the depth of the deposit is not known at this time, at least one artifact dating to the mid-nineteenth century, a bottle, has been recovered at the mouth of the cave. The site was assigned the trinomial CA-SNI-551. Although there may have been more than one habitable cave on the island (Schwartz 2012b), only the one at site CA-SNI-551 is known to be in the vicinity of Cave Station.

Forney's awareness of the lone woman and her cave residence likely came from the fur hunters who had been on the island with her. Nidever served as a ship's captain and pilot for USCS surveys of the Channel Islands and, partly because of his knowledge of the area, he had a longstanding relationship with the USCS that began in 1850 (Lawson ca. 1880). USCS Santa Barbara office supervisor William Greenwell's wife was likely the "Mrs. Greenwell" Emma Hardacre consulted in her historical study of the lone woman that she began in the 1870s (Hudson 1981). Because of USCS ties to Nidever and others who were on the island in 1853, the Cave Station records are sufficient to establish the location of the cave. The USCS survey data combined with Schwartz's research on early reports of the cave are sufficient for this location to be considered a historical site of unique significance.

Archaeological Mound Sites

On the central and southern California coast, the USCS mapped several abandoned Native American villages. Some were described as shell mounds, and these were often mapped with topographic details. Many of the mounds may have been ceremonial sites rather than villages (Lightfoot 1997; Luby et al. 2006). Some abandoned villages lacked mounds but were identified as Native rancherías based on the presence of house pits and Native American artifacts. The more obvious mounds are often depicted in detail topographically, particularly if they were used as platforms for USCS survey stations.

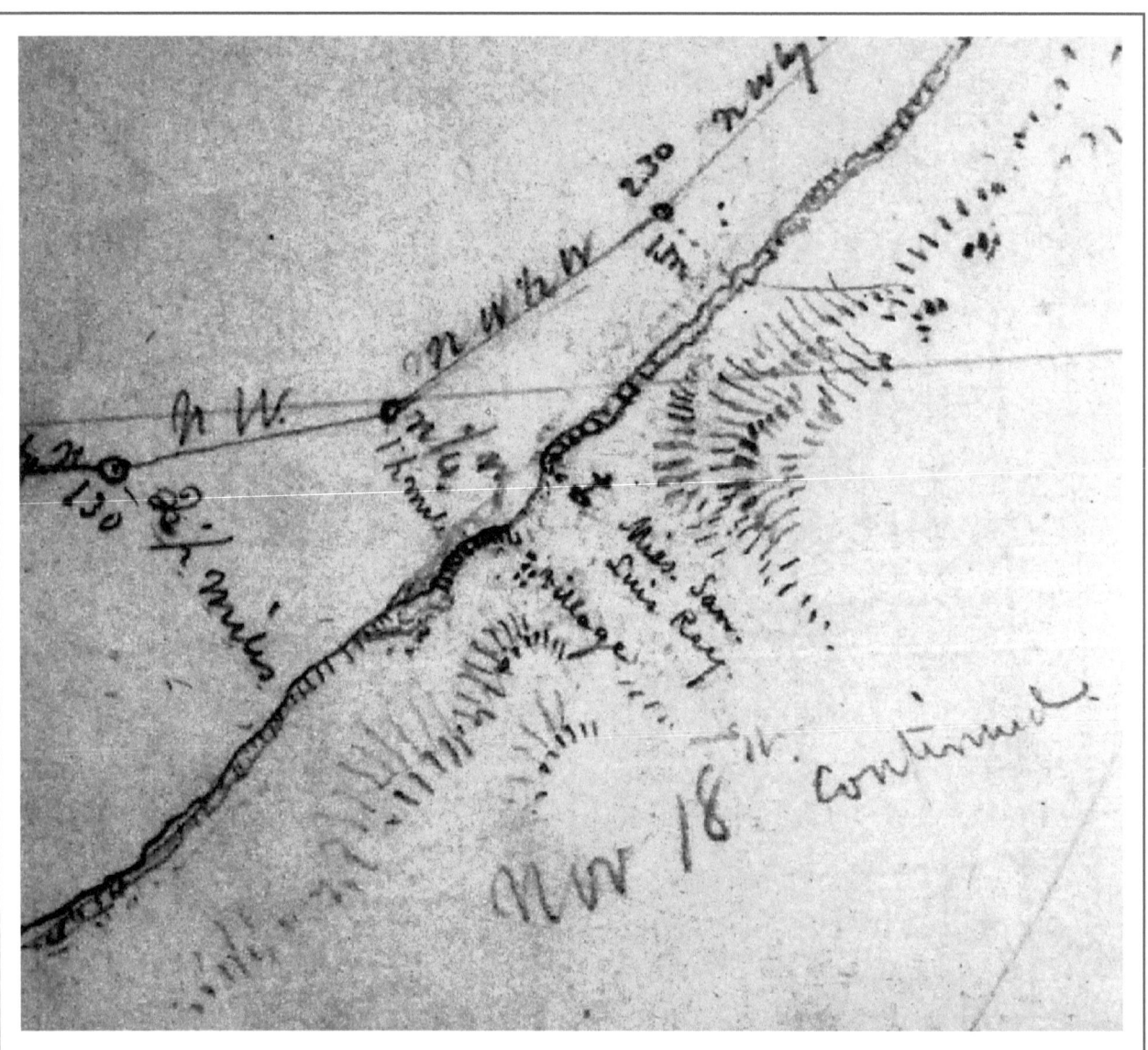

Figure 37   1851 Alden sketch of the coastline at Mission San Luis Rey showing one of the nearby Native American villages across the valley to the south. (GAR Series, RG 23; photographed by author at NARA II.)

The perspectives of USCS surveyors on these archaeological sites paralleled and was influenced by the development of archaeology during the nineteenth century. Squier and Davis (1848) published a major Smithsonian report on mounds of the Mississippi and Ohio River valleys in 1848, and Thomas Jefferson's (1955) much earlier and well-known *Notes on the State of Virginia* included accounts of mounds and their excavation. In California, Agostin Haraszthy (1859:315) had published references to shell mounds as preferred locations for establishing vineyards because of their soil. At least one cadastral surveyor, Leander Ransom (1873:86) also documented California mound sites in the 1850s, including detailed measurements of a mound cluster later recorded by Nelson (1907) near San Rafael. The awareness of these sites

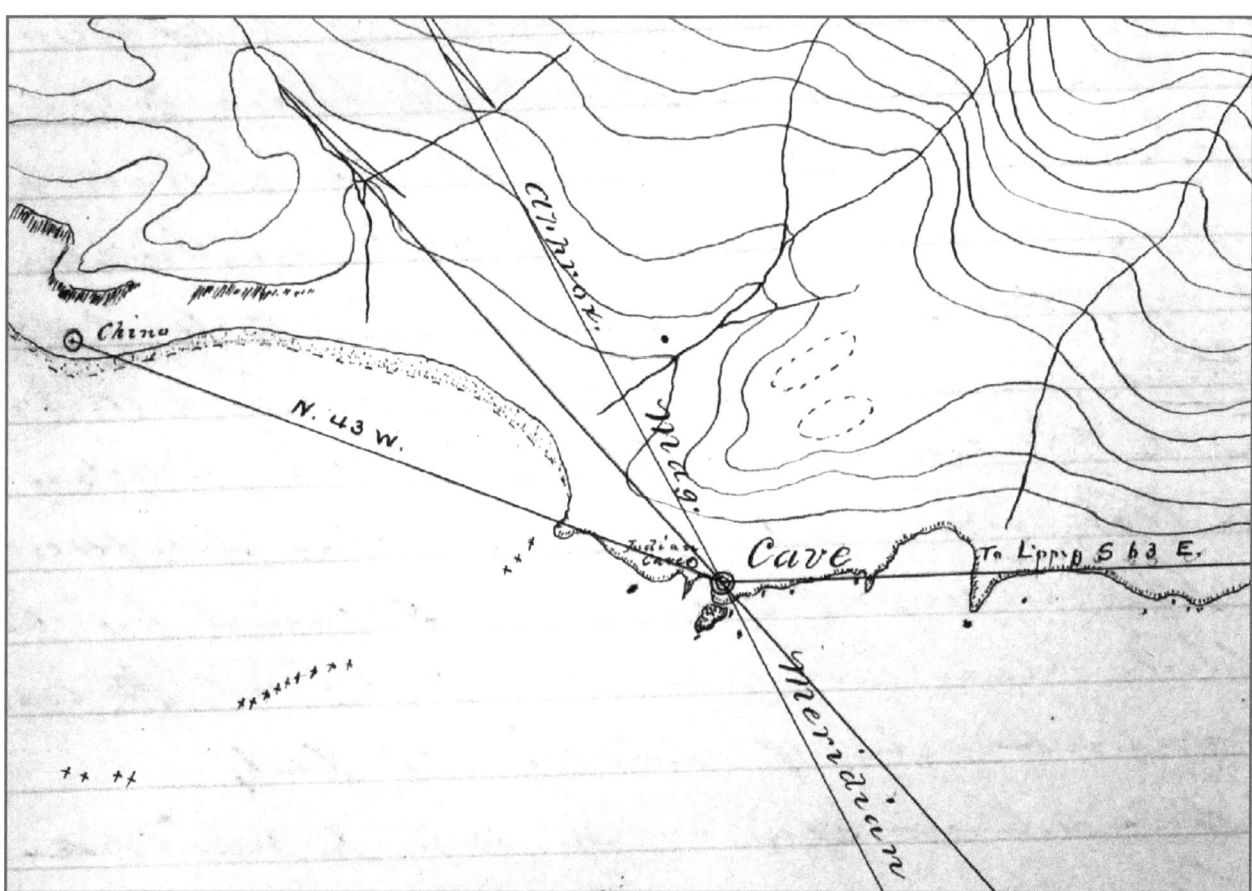

Figure 38 Portion of a map in Forney's (1879) San Nicolas Island field notebook showing the location of the "Indian Cave." Chino Station appears at the left; straight lines are angles drawn from the position of Cave Station. (Photographed by author at NARA II.)

grew through the 1860s, and shell mounds on the California coast were actively being looted by collectors. Also in the 1860s, scholars with the California Academy of Sciences (CAS) began to lecture on the mounds, some advocating their excavation and others the preservation of these California sites. USCS surveyor George Davidson headed the CAS during this period. Davidson's assistant James Lawson began describing shell mounds and house pits in reference to mapping stations as early as 1861, when he documented multiple Native American sites at Coos Bay on the southern Oregon coast (Lawson 1861).

In areas of urban development, farming, or road corridors, the mounds that the USCS depicted were in most cases leveled, removed, buried by fill, or otherwise changed after they were mapped but before they were examined by early twentieth-century archaeologists. Thus the Coast Survey records are important for understanding the scale of Native American residence and other activities along shoreline areas. Some mounds are shown to have undergone gradual attrition beginning in the 1850s. For example, Burton Mound (CA-SBA-28)

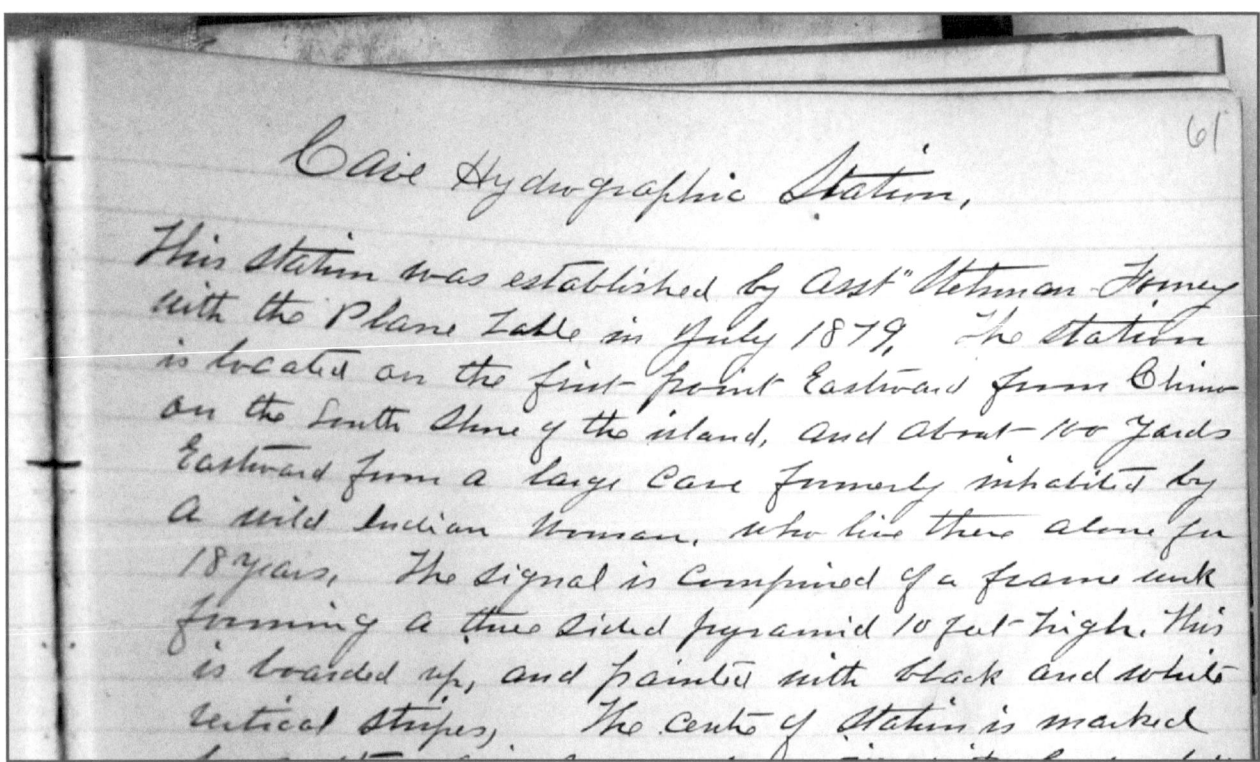

Figure 39 Forney's (1879) description of Cave Station and the nearby cave where the lone woman reportedly resided. (Photographed by author at NARA II.)

was a prominent topographic feature with a small, elevated terrace when the USCS first mapped the Santa Barbara area in 1852 (T-sheet no. 373; Harrison 1853) (Figure 36). The mound's terrace expanded as its elevation was lowered by its increasing use for agriculture, parkland, a hotel, and residences (T-sheets nos. 1229a and 4848).

Coast Survey records indicate that San Nicolas Island mound sites underwent substantial changes prior to formal archaeological mapping in the 1950s. One mound was used as the location of Shell Station by Stehman Forney (1879). It was approximately 22 ft. high with steep sides on the north and south, yet it was smaller in area than some nearby mounds (Figure 11). Modern site records (Martz 2008:54) show that disbursed shell midden is present in the area, but it is heavily disturbed. According to navy archaeologist Steven Schwartz (personal communication 2010) there is a road cut in the vicinity of what would have been the mound site. Construction of this road may have removed most of the shell mound, but sea lion haul-outs may also have contributed to site erosion.

A mound at Ridge Station on San Nicolas was mapped by Forney in 1879, but in 1908 traces of the "old shell mound around the Station" were no longer present (Kurtz, in Forney 1879). This location corresponds to a portion of site CA-SNI-344 that was graded in the 1960s (Steve Schwartz, personal communication 2012). Station Slope 2 was an "old shell mound" situated on a bench on the higher terrace of the island. In 1908 surveyors observed evidence of heavy wind erosion at the station. "There is no shell mound over the station at present but traces of an old one to the north and east, which confirm the opinion that the mound has shifted and left the (sub)surface mark, which was buried in hard clay ... (to 18 inches) ... exposed" (Kurtz, in Forney 1879). According to Schwartz (personal communication 2012) the Slope 2 location is now a blown-out area between sites CA-MRN-30 and CA-MRN-81. Modern archaeological observations combined with early surveyor records thus indicate that these two sites were once part of a single site, with a low shell mound in the vicinity of the station.

The remains of a shell mound at what is now Torrey Pines Golf Course in San Diego were documented by A. F. Rodgers of the USCS in 1887 (Figure 12). Rodgers (1887) named the survey station Shell Mound. He described shell fragments being present across its surface, and depicted the mound on T-sheet no. 2017 as at least 30 x 20 m in area. Rodgers was very familiar with archaeological shell mounds by this time, having surveyed the subdivision of the Shell Mound Tract in Alameda and having mapped shell mounds in other parts of the state. The first formal archaeological survey of Shell Mound Station site was conducted by Malcolm Rogers of the San Diego Museum of Man in 1929. By that time the site was already extensively impacted by construction. These and subsequent archaeological surveys of the area (Mealey 2009) led to the designation of Shell Mound Station as site CA-SDI-200, but none of the twentieth-century surveys benefited from the findings recorded during Rodgers's 1887 USCGS survey.

Like many former mound sites, a shallow scattering of shell and fire-cracked rock is primarily what remained after the mound at SDI-200 was removed between 1887 and 1929. Much shell may have been taken for construction of the Torrey Pines Park Road in 1915.

This road, listed on the National Register of Historic Places (NRHP), was made of concrete that incorporated a large amount of fragmented shell (Marla Mealey, personal communication 2011). This was a period when numerous Pacific coast roads were constructed using shell from archaeological middens, dredged materials, and bayshore shoal deposits (Byram 2009b; Lightfoot 1997).

Some mounds mapped by the USCS may have been lost due to shoreline retreat before they were visited by archaeologists. Mound Station (Figure 17), near Loon Point and Summerland on the Santa Barbara County coast, was mapped in 1863 by William Greenwell (1862–1863). The mound and station are also shown on T-sheet no. 1128 (1869), but the station's coordinates do not appear in the USCGS inventory for southern California stations (Baldwin 1904). Due to sea cliff retreat, in 1927 the USCGS established a new triangulation station named Loon near the former location of Mound Station. In the 1890s several short-lived oil drilling piers were in place along the coast at Summerland, and this may have changed shoreline currents and eroded Mound Station prior to Baldwin's inventory and the placement of Loon Station in 1927. Rapid twentieth-century sea cliff erosion was documented for the general area (California Department of Boating and Waterways and State Coastal Conservancy 2002:8–30), and it appears the mound was entirely lost to erosion and possibly other factors such as agriculture or residential landscaping. Irregular rates of erosion could relate to climate patterns affecting sand deposits, waves, and currents, as well as the presence of riprap and other structures (Komar 1997). National Geodetic Survey records for Loon Station indicate there was no measurable bluff erosion from 1927 to 1932, but by 1958 there had been 7 ft. of bluff loss at the station, and a total of 9 ft. two years later (Lareau 1984). By 1984 a total of 13 ft. of bluff had eroded, leaving Loon only 1.5 ft. from the edge. The late nineteenth-century erosion may have been at a comparable rate to that seen between 1958 and 1984. Additionally, Greenwell's Mound Station topographic map indicates the mound may have undergone substantial shoreward erosion by the early 1860s.

Mound Station also appears on the 1872 T-sheet no. 1128, but its full dimensions are only evident in the station map. This shore-parallel topographic feature was located adjacent to the sea cliff, and while Greenwell did not report archaeological materials or even shell in this mound, it was most likely cultural. The Holocene alluvial geomorphology of this setting (Keller and Gurolla 2000:19) does not account for a narrow, shore-parallel knoll, and there is no remnant rock outcrop exposed in the sea cliff at what was Mound Station. At least one recorded village site in the area is thought to be historic and late precontact (Gamble 2011:97). If it was archaeological, the mound mapped by Greenwell was likely an important component in a complex of shoreline sites in this area.

While Nels Nelson (1907, 1909) is often considered the first to map numerous shell mounds in the vicinity of San Francisco Bay, the USCS preceded him by over half a century in several instances. Although their maps and field notes lack the focus on archaeological materials that Nelson had, the surveyors often depicted mound topography and settings in varying detail prior to the impacts that preceded Nelson's work. For example, the 1852 Cutts map of Sausalito (Figure 16) shows a large mound, defined by hachures rather than contour lines, at the Richardson Rancho. The map is oriented with south at the top. This mounded

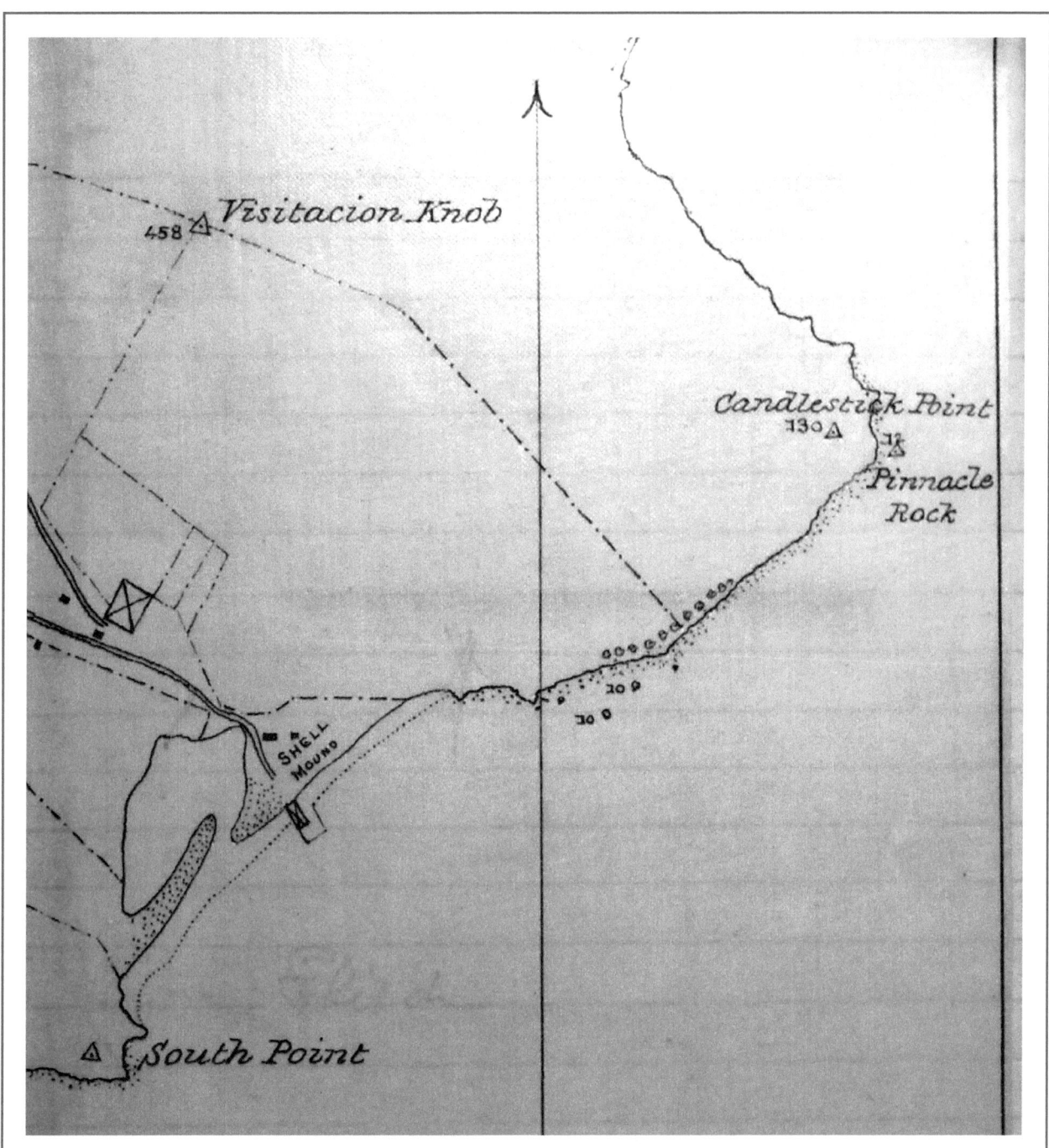

Figure 40   Rodgers's (1894–1896) map of Visitacion Knob, South Point, and Candlestick Point on the San Francisco Peninsula, with a shell mound labeled at Candlestick Cove. This is evidently the location of Bayshore Mound excavated by Nelson and the University of California, Berkeley, in 1910–1911. (Photographed by author at NARA II.)

site was documented 55 years later by Nelson (1907) as Shellmound 3 in Marin County (site CA-MRN-3), evidently extending south into the vicinity of the ranch buildings, an area that Cutts had delineated with a topographic contour rather than hachures. Cutts may have seen the southern half of the mounded site as a spur ridge and the northern half as an earthwork. The site had clearly been decimated by looting and construction between Cutts's 1851–1852 visit and Nelson's 1909 visit. The retreat of this topography can also be seen in US Geological Survey topographic maps from 1895 to 1915, as the mound was gradually removed. Based on intact remnants of the site and interviews with local residents, Nelson was able to estimate the size of the mound at 650 x 325 ft. Taken together, Nelson's observations of the southern site area and the Cutts map of the northern part of the mound indicate that Nelson's estimate was relatively accurate, though its shape on the Cutts map, suggestive of two contiguous mounds, varies from Nelson's rendering.

For the most part, Bay Area mounds mapped by the USCS were not described as historical Native American sites in the initial episodes of triangulation and topographic work. This may be due in part to the early dates of many of the Bay Area triangulation surveys, predating scientists' discussions of shell mounds as distinctive earthworks in the region. In contrast, mounds mapped in the 1860s or later from Oregon to southern California were often identified as such. However, many of the early maps drawn by Richard Cutts or his assistants in the 1850s do show mound perimeters delineated with hachures instead of the topographic contour lines he used for noncultural topography. It is possible that Cutts was using hachures to depict what he interpreted as earthworks rather than noncultural features.

Cutts was likely familiar with the earthen mound sites of the southeast. His wife, Martha Jefferson Hackley, was Thomas Jefferson's granddaughter, and her family home was Monticello, near the mounds Jefferson had mapped and excavated years before (Jefferson 1955; Thomas Jefferson Foundation 2005). By using hachures to delineate mounds, Cutts may have been following the procedures of Squier and Davis (1848), with which he was likely familiar, as well as architectural and military earthwork map standards of the era.

Many of the Bay Area mound sites Cutts mapped were later recognized by Nels Nelson or other archaeologists, though often after being severely reduced in size. Several of the Bay Area mounds depicted topographically on early T-sheets were later removed or leveled and buried by construction, such as Nelson's Mound 257 at Tormey (formerly Oleum), mound site CA-ALA-307 at West Berkeley, and mound site CA-ALA-309 at Emeryville. This is also the case for mound sites detailed in USCS field notebooks such as CA-MRN-3 at Sausalito and the mound at or near site CA-CCO-295 at Ellis Landing (Figure 10). In some cases the early maps provide the only record of the original size and shape of the mounds.

In later nineteenth-century USCS records for the Bay Area, shell mounds were often identified as such in field notes or on maps. What appears to have been Bayshore Mound (CA-SFR-7) at Candlestick Cove (Figure 40) was mapped by Rodgers (1894–1896) some 15 years before Nelson excavated there. Rodgers plotted the site on his station map of Visitacion Knob, South Point, and Candlestick Point using the notation "shell mound." Two January 1911 news articles (Oakland Tribune 1911; San Francisco Call 1911) indicate that Nelson and anthropology students from UC Berkeley were excavating there at what was the "bayshore" terminus of San Bruno Road. The mound on Rodgers's map is in the same location as a large, intact mound on Nelson's (1909) map of Bay Area shell mounds, and the Candlestick Cove map provides important details about the setting before it was covered by fill for urban expansion. Cutts's 1852 T-sheet of the area does not show mound hachures at this location, suggesting it was a low mound or one cloaked by vegetation and not recognized as a large earthwork by the early survey team.

USCS maps are often detailed enough to estimate general mound dimensions prior to erosion and development impacts. For example, topographic contours on the 1856 T-sheet no. 562 show the perimeter of Mound 257 at Tormey and the top of the mound as having an elevation of 100 ft. Nelson (1907) had recorded this site solely on the basis of information from local residents who had seen the mound before it was razed for the construction of oil tank platforms. In the case of Cutts's 1851–1852 map of Contra Costa 4 Station showing a large mound at or near Ellis Landing, questions about the marsh setting are clarified by the station map. The collection also shows that numerous shoreline mounds were used as landings in the nineteenth century, which ironically may have contributed to the preservation of some that would have otherwise been looted or mined for farm soil and road surfacing material.

Two likely mounds depicted in USCS field notes have not previously been identified as archaeological. One of these localities was Seal Bluff (Figures 24 and 25). Seal Bluff Landing has been referred to as a "small rise of dry land in the Suisun wetland" (McLeod 2007:24). However Greenwell's 1864 drawing, notes, and plan map of this topographic feature show that it was a large, dome-shaped knoll. The most likely explanation for such a knoll in this wetland setting is that it was a Native American mounded site. There is no shallow geological substrate in this area other than wetland sediments and fill (Dibblee 1981), and the bluff sediment was friable and undergoing rapid erosion in the 1860s and 1870s, such that the survey station had to be moved. By the late nineteenth century when the bluff was developed for the Copper King smelter, the erosion had been stabilized. By the time Nelson surveyed Bay Area shorelines for archaeological mounds, the bluff had been buried by industrial development fill.

Another likely mound was known as Little Coyote Point, mapped by Cutts in 1852 (Figure 41). This topographic feature, also known as Guano Island, was located at what is now the western terminus of the San Mateo Bridge across San Francisco Bay. Cutts's (1851–1852) notes indicate it had the dimensions of a shell mound, and there is no geological explanation for a 26 ft. high topographic feature 100 x 50 m at the base to emerge in this area of tidal marsh sediments at that time. Assistant Fairfield (1907) revisited Little Coyote Point 55 years later. Although he did not identify it as a shell mound, he described it as "a very peculiar formation rising out of the marsh on what is now the Brewer Ranch." After locating Cutts's 1851–1852 survey marker and excavating a pit for a concrete replacement, Fairfield noted the promontory was "composed of very good road building material, and it is only a question of a few years (when) the whole island will have been carted away." Little Coyote Point remained intact longer than many shell mounds mined for roads or gardening soil, but in 1928 it was dynamited by a dredge company and its upper layers removed for bridge construction (San Mateo Times and Daily News Leader 1929). According to news reports, the

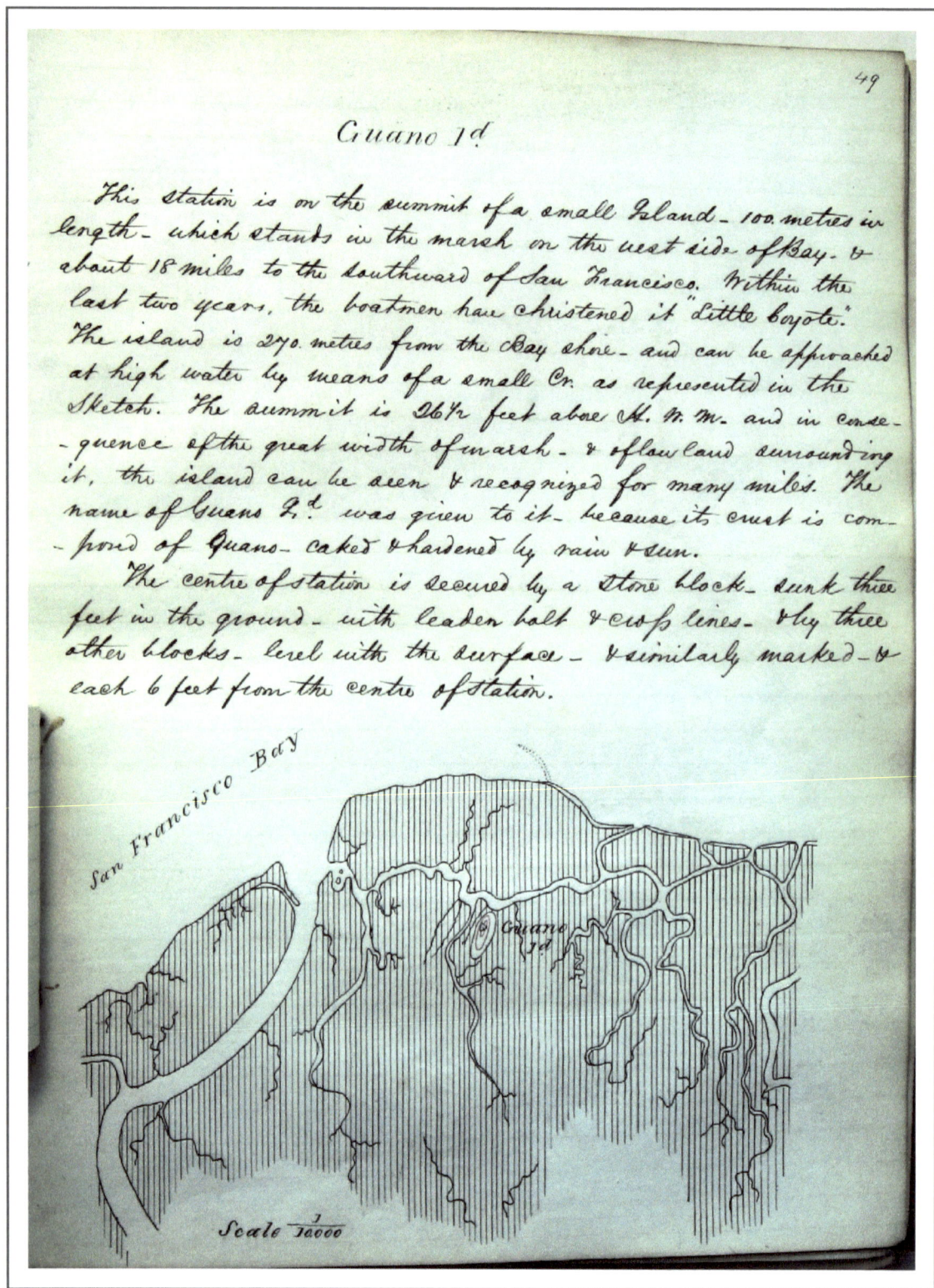

Figure 41 Cutts's (1851–1852) description and map of Guano Island, or Little Coyote Point. The dimensions, composition, and location reported for this landform suggest that it was an archaeological mound. The location is now the western terminus of the San Mateo Bridge in Foster City. (Photographed by author at NARA II.)

blasting was said to be necessary because the formation was composed of rock to a depth of 40 ft. Yet with several newsreel cameras documenting its removal as part of what was touted at the time as the construction of the longest bridge in the world, it is more likely that the decision to use dynamite was made to avoid any filming of the steam shoveling of a large Native American site. Bridge engineering records in War Department archives may hold more details about the sedimentary composition of this likely mound site.

It is perplexing that so little was drawn from the USCS and USCGS manuscript maps and field notes in early twentieth-century studies of California mound sites. Prior to the work of University of California archaeologists in the early 1900s, the California Academy of Sciences (CAS) was a locus of mound site inquiry, and among its members were USCS surveyors and others who took part in agency surveys, such as George Kellog (Daniel 2008:218). In the 1850s and 1860s the CAS antiquarians began studying mound sites, shipwrecks, and other archaeological sites, and some of these efforts involved the work of surveyors (California Academy of Sciences 1873:83, 124, 283; Stearns 1873). George Davidson oversaw the CAS while members were conducting mound excavations, and some of his USCS staff, such as James Lawson and Louis Sengteller, were among the contributors to CAS collections for decades. Early studies by CAS members Leander Ransom (1873), James Blake (California Academy of Sciences 1873:12), W. E. Saxe (1875), and others documented the dimensions and composition of several central California mounds. Some CAS mound investigations occurred during the period of initial UC Berkeley studies on this topic (San Francisco Call 1892, 1894). Yet Nelson and other early anthropological archaeologists appear not to have cited the literature prepared by their neighboring CAS colleagues, nor did they cite the USCS records at the CAS library or in holdings of the West Coast USCS office in nearby San Francisco.

There may have been multiple factors involved in this omission. George Davidson was the strongest link between the USCS and UC Berkeley. Although his many scientific articles include several about exploration landfalls on the Pacific coast, and he documented Native American place-names and other Native history, he does not seem to have had a research interest in mounds or most other types of archaeological sites. In fact, Davidson was known to have dissuaded members of his USCS staff from pursuing archaeological investigations while on survey (Garcia 2010). His dismissal from the agency in 1895, shortly before mound research began in earnest at UC Berkeley, may also have been a factor. It is not clear how accessible the USCS manuscripts may have been to UC Berkeley anthropologists. After his controversial departure from the agency in 1895, Davidson held on to his extensive collection of USCS records. These did not become part of the Bancroft Library collection until they were donated by his daughter in 1945 (Bancroft Library MSS-CB-490).

Many of the USCS records shared with the CAS would have also been archived at the Society's library in the California Academy of Sciences building on Market Street after 1891. But the library was completely destroyed in the fire caused by the great earthquake of 1906, just at the time when Nelson began his extensive Bay Area mound research. Originals and

Table 4 Archaeologically recorded Native American sites updated with USCS records.

Trinomial or National Register Type	Name	County	Site Type	Primary Records	Archaeological Information
CA-SNI-551	Lone Woman's Cave	Ventura	cave/residence	Forney (1879)	location of cave and association with lone woman
CA-SFR-7	Bayshore Mound	San Francisco	mounded site	Rodgers (1894–1896)	location and setting of shell mound
35-CU-42	Tcet-xo Village	Curry (OR)	village	Chart 5900 (1891)	layout of village after 1850s rebuild; steam sawmill and setting
CS-MRN-3	Mound 3 Sausalito	Marin	mounded site	Cutts (1851–1852)	perimeter of two contiguous mounds
CA-CCO-295	Ellis Landing	Contra Costa	mounded site	Cutts 1851–1852: Contra Costa 4 Sta.	marsh setting and outline of large mound
CA-SBA-28	Burton Mound	Santa Barbara	mounded site	Harrison (1853); T-sheet no. 373 (1852)	extent of mound and gradual reduction due to development
CA-CCO-257	Tormey Mound	Contra Costa	mounded site	T-sheet no. 562 (1856)	mound perimeter and height; supports Nelson's (1907) informant account

Table 5 Native American archaeological sites identified by the USCS.

Trinomial or National Register Type	Name	County	Site Type	Primary Records	Archaeological Information
CA-SDI-200	Shell Mound	San Diego	shell mound	Rodgers (1887b); T-sheet no. 2017	shell mound at site later documented as lithic scatter
CA-SNI-74	no site name	Ventura	shell mound	Forney (1879); T-sheet no. 1523, Shell Station	scale profile drawing and description of large mound
CA-SNI-344	no site name	Ventura	shell mound	Forney (1879); T-sheet no. 1523, Ridge Station	documents loss of shell mound due to erosion
CA-SNI-30/81	no site name	Ventura	shell mound	Forney (1879); T-sheet no. 1523, Slope 2 Station	documents loss of shell mound due to erosion
no site record	Pony Point Mound	Coos (OR)	shell mound, pits	Lawson (1861); T-sheet no. 927 (1863), Pony Station	shell mound, house pit at bayshore location

Table 6 Precontact and Mission-era sites.

Trinomial or National Register Type	Name	County	Site Type	Primary Records	Archaeological Information
National Memorial	Seal Bluff	Contra Costa	possible mound	Greenwell (1866)	depicts likely shell mound
no site record	Little Coyote Point	San Mateo	possible mound	Cutts (1851–1852): Guano Island Station	depicts likely shell mound; also see Fairfield (1907)
no site record	Loon Point mound	Santa Barbara	possible mound	T-sheet no. 1128 (1869), Mound Station	shore-parallel mound later lost to erosion or construction
CA Landmark 373	Engva	Los Angeles	possible village	Greenwell (1855–1860)	village area mapped one year after residents removed to mission
unknown	Luiseño	San Diego	village structures	Alden (ca. 1851)	village near Mission San Luis Rey depicted

duplicates of many field notebooks and plane table maps remained in the holdings of the USCGS offices, including at the headquarters in Washington, DC, but these records were less accessible to California archaeologists.

The sites discussed in this chapter are summarized in Tables 4, 5, and 6. Table 4 includes sites that are archaeologically recorded and discussed in published reports. Information from USCS records that updates previous records about these sites is summarized in each table entry. Table 5 lists Native American sites with large components or features that were identified as archaeological by the USCS, but may not be part of modern archaeological inventories. Much or all of each of these sites or site components has been lost to erosion or buried by construction fill. Table 6 includes other locations discussed in this chapter that may or may not have archaeological components elucidated by USCS maps and field notes.

Chapter 5
THE REDISCOVERY OF CAMP CASTAWAY AND THE WRECK OF THE *CAPTAIN LINCOLN*

On July 20, 1861, at Bull Run in Manassas, Virginia, Union soldiers spent a last day in camp before the first major land battle of the Civil War. During the war most USCS surveyors were assigned to support operations of the Union army and navy (Theberge 2011). But not all survey staff were enlisted. On the opposite shore of the continent Assistant James Lawson and his US Coast Survey team spent July 20th setting up a theodolite position at the site of an earlier military encampment. They chose the name Wreck Station for this survey position, reflecting the scattered remains of a shipwreck and camp that had been abandoned there some years before. Lawson didn't realize it at the time, but Wreck Station was located on the site of Camp Castaway, a winter encampment of the US 1st Dragoons Company C, predecessors to the US Cavalry.

The soldiers established the camp after the harrowing wreck of the US transport schooner *Captain Lincoln* on the storm-swept shore of the vast Oregon dunes on the night of January 2nd, 1852. Remarkably, all of the roughly 35 troops, the ship's crew, two dogs, and much of the cargo survived the shipwreck. No US settlement was yet present at nearby Coos Bay or elsewhere on the coast between the Umpqua River to the north and Fort Orford to the south. The soldiers offloaded many crates of supplies from the beached vessel, and salvaged spars, booms, and sails to make large tents that they used for lodging and to protect the valuable supplies destined for Fort Orford. They named the temporary settlement Camp Castaway. The camp endured for four months in the windswept dunes, in large part due to assistance from Coos Bay Indians, whose trade allowed the soldiers and sailors to subsist through the winter.

Much of what we know about the wreck of the *Captain Lincoln* and Camp Castaway comes from a contemporary report of the US Army Quartermaster's Department that details the efforts to retrieve the ship's valuable cargo (Miller 1852). There are also written memoirs by Camp Castaway soldiers Henry Baldwin and Philip Brack, who settled near Coos Bay and later recounted their experiences for a volume on local history (Dodge 1898). Oral tradition of the Native American experience at the camp was depicted by Coquille elder Beverly Ward (1986:47).

Lieutenant Henry Stanton, the commanding officer of the troops at the camp, sent twelve men south along the coast to Fort Orford to open communication with the military command in Benicia, California. The dragoons remained at the fort until late April, awaiting the storm-delayed arrival of quartermaster Captain Morris Miller with 20 mules. After the party returned to the camp with Miller, the soldiers obtained wagons at the Umpqua River and transported the ship's cargo across the dunes to the bay shore, where they loaded it onto a chartered schooner for transport by sea to Fort Orford. The troops traveled overland to the fort, finally ending their indirect journey on May 12.

The establishment of Camp Castaway was an important event in Oregon coast history and also Gold Rush military history, affecting the course of US settlement in the region and Native American–US relations (Douthit 2002). Despite its historical importance and archaeological potential, the camp's location remained hidden for over a century. The last wooden ship remains had rotted into the dunes within a generation or two after the camp was abandoned. Historian Stephen Beckham (1974) prepared documents on the site for a National Register of Historic Places nomination, but at the time it was not known if archaeological remains were present in the dunes or if the site had been washed away by ocean waves. Its actual location had become a matter of much dispute. Over the years local residents have walked the shifting dunes searching for signs of the 1852 camp, but the scarcity of Gold Rush–era artifacts in the dunes led many to conclude that the camp was washed away by high seas and shoreline erosion, or buried by migrating dunes.

US Coast Survey Maps

One hundred and sixty years after Camp Castaway was abandoned, the Coast Survey maps and notes recorded by Lawson's team (Figure 42) allowed archaeologists to relocate the camp and hardware from the wreck of the schooner *Captain Lincoln* on the North Spit of Coos Bay.

Lawson's (1861) observations of the site were made nearly a decade after the wreck of the *Captain Lincoln*, and he is the only person known to have recorded details of Camp Castaway after it was abandoned. He noted that Wreck Station was

> on the ocean beach of the Peninsula upon a small sand hill, near which are the remains of an old lodge, and scattered around are portions of the wreck of a vessel. The position of the station is between two higher sand hills, covered with grass, and was selected because it was the only spot from which could be seen stations, "Martin," "Kinny," and "Woodland."

Lawson began as a West Coast surveyor for the USCS in 1850 (Lawson ca. 1880; Theberge 2006, 2011). With several years experience surveying the West Coast for the US Coast Survey, he was familiar with shipwrecks and many other types of coastal sites. Yet he was evidently unaware that he was describing the short-lived 1st Dragoons encampment of 1852. He did not connect the vessel remains with the wreck of the *Captain Lincoln*, and his description did not name it or otherwise specify its origin. Shipwrecks were common on the rugged coast of Oregon and northern California in the 1850s and 1860s, and it appears that Lawson simply referenced the shipwreck remains and structure as a means of positioning the survey marker in the dunes so later surveyors might be able to relocate this position.

Lawson's observations are useful for interpreting the archaeological site. The "old lodge" may have been a structure that was part of the camp. Alternatively this may have been a Native American structure built at the site after the soldiers abandoned the camp in May 1852. Lawson's depiction of the nearby dunes as grass covered is also relevant. Resource managers and historians have generally considered most of the shoreline dunes in this region to have been largely grass-free until the Army Corps of Engineers systematically introduced European dune grass to stabilize the sand beginning in 1890 (Beckham 2000:60; Komar 1997). Baldwin and Brack each recalled only barren dunes in the vicinity of the camp in 1852 (Dodge 1898). Perhaps the feed for the 20

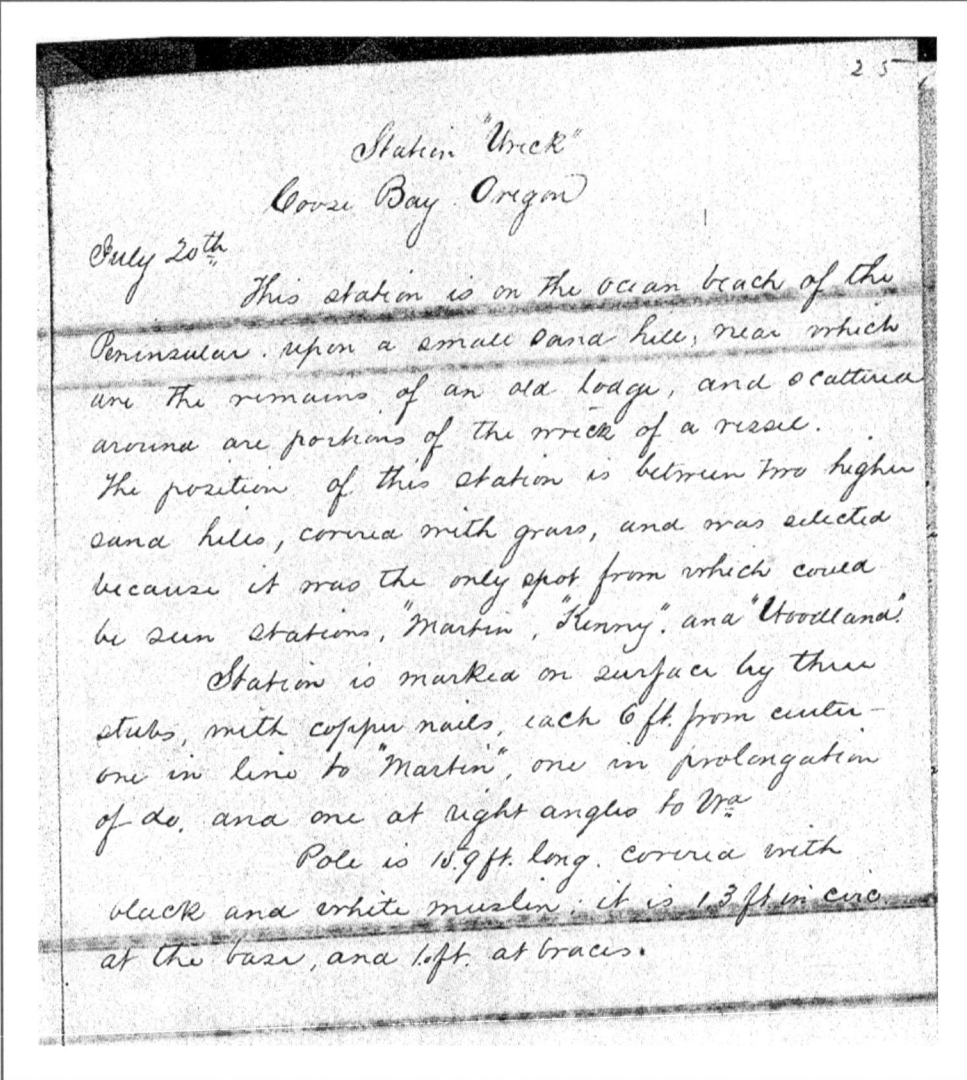

Figure 42 Page from James Lawson's (1861) field notebook describing Wreck Station at what was later determined to be Camp Castaway (35-CS-277). (Scanned by the author at NARA II in 1997; horizontal bands produced by the scanning equipment.)

mules brought into the camp from Fort Orford in 1852 introduced grasses that spread in the vicinity over the next decade. The grass cover may have kept the dunes at the site more stable than most dunes in the area, which are prone to shifting, causing deflation of archaeological materials.

While Lawson's observations of the shipwreck camp in 1861 are of value in understanding the site, his description alone does not provide what an archaeologist would need to relocate the camp. The greatest value of Lawson's record is in providing a mapped location of the site. The site's position remained obscure for over a decade after I first read the Wreck Station description at the National Archives. Lawson's handwritten description was among a set of Coast Survey field notes and maps I scanned, photocopied, and provided to Coos County Indian tribes in 1997 for use by their cultural resource programs. Wreck Station was one of the few stations that Lawson did not plot on his

1863 T-sheet no. 927, a large, detailed manuscript map of Coos Bay made in the field with a plane table.

It was not until 2009, during another trip to the National Archives for research on a different Coos Bay North Spit project, that I was able to plot Wreck Station. During my previous visits to the archives, I had not examined T-sheet no. 846, but in 2009 I acquired a scan of the map and found the details needed to locate this elusive survey station. T-sheet no. 846 showed the entrance to Coos Bay (which Lawson spelled Koose) and more details of the North Spit. The map showed the locations of nearby stations Dash, Garden, Kinny, and others, but there was nothing labeled as Wreck Station. However, I noticed that there was an unlabeled mapping station triangle near the ocean shore of the North Spit across from what was once the town of Empire, now part of the city of Coos Bay. Returning to Lawson's 1861 field notes, I saw that Wreck Station was the first station south of Dash Station. The unlabeled station matched the position of Wreck based on this description. While there could have been another unlabeled station on this portion of the shore, it seemed most likely that the unlabeled mapping station triangle on T-sheet no. 846 was in fact Wreck Station.

Unlike California, comprehensive mapping station coordinates for Oregon had not been published in USCGS annual reports, and triangulation coordinate data for the state were not known to archivists at NOAA or NARA II at the time (though they have since been identified). Though there was limited overlap in coverage between the two T-sheets (no. 846 depicted the entrance to the bay and the North Spit, while no. 927 depicted the main portion of the bay and its shoreline), there were enough mapping stations that appeared on both maps that I was able to do a GIS overlay with the two. This allowed me to plot the location of Wreck Station relative to known survey markers with published coordinates. These positions allowed the map overlay to be positioned accurately, leading to relatively accurate coordinates for Wreck Station.

Site Survey: 2010–2011

To test my map analysis results, I entered the coordinates of the location into my GPS unit and visited the area in March 2010. A brief surface survey led to identification of a small number of sand-polished iron fragments and one cobble of nonlocal origin, possibly a ballast stone. This was far from conclusive evidence, but enough to suggest the presence of a buried site. Bureau of Land Management archaeologist Steve Samuels was interested in my findings, as the BLM administered the federal land in this portion of the Oregon dunes. We were not able to visit the site again until the summer of 2011. Accompanied by archaeologist Reg Pullen, the three of us identified ceramic dish fragments and more weathered iron on the surface. Based on these traces, we planned subsurface testing for August 2011.

For this effort I used a GSSI SIR-3000 ground penetrating radar unit in "cross-country" (non-grid) mode to identify several buried objects (Figure 43), and we concentrated shovel probes at these locations and in areas of surface metal. Along with Mike Knight and tribal archaeologist Agnes Castronuevo, Steve and I excavated shovel probes and one test unit, which established that there were numerous small, near-surface metal artifacts not visible to surface survey and likely dating to the era of the shipwreck. These included copper nails and percussion caps from muskets, glass, and band iron fragments, some containing rivets. Most Gold Rush–era sites would be expected to hold more glass and

Figure 43 The author using ground-penetrating radar to locate buried structural artifacts from the schooner *Captain Lincoln* at Camp Castaway (35-CS-277). (Photo by Mark Tveskov.)

Figure 44 Camp Castaway excavation, 2012. (Photo by the author.)

ceramics, but a review of Miller's (1852) quartermaster's report indicates that except for medicines and personal belongings, food and drink were generally stored in wooden kegs in the cargo the troops salvaged from the *Captain Lincoln* rather than in bottles and jugs. We also surmised that bottles and glass fragments might have had value as trade goods with Coos Bay Indians at the time, which may partially account for the paucity of siliceous vessel materials.

The assemblage is consistent with our interpretation of the site as a pre–Civil War shipwreck camp based on archival records and historical accounts. Subsequent to this fieldwork, NOAA Central Library historian John Cloud identified records, including the coordinates of Wreck Station and an inset triangulation map that labels the station, confirming the inferred position. Remarkably, the archived coordinates based on Lawson's survey plot the station some 40 m west of the area where artifacts were recovered in 2011. Together, the distinctive assemblage and Lawson's account of shipwreck remains and a lodge at this location 150 years before supported the conclusion that this is the site of Camp Castaway.

More extensive archaeological excavations took place in the summer of 2012 under the direction of Professor Mark Tveskov of Southern Oregon University (Figures 44 and 45). The SOU team has previously excavated Fort Lane, a site associated with the same troop of US Dragoons in southwest Oregon (Tveskov and Cohen 2008). Maritime archaeological analysis and archival research are being conducted by James Delgado and Robert Schwemmer of the NOAA Maritime Heritage program, as NOAA is the legacy agency

Figure 45 Mark Tveskov and students from Southern Oregon University along with team members from the Coquille Indian Tribe and the Confederated Tribes of Coos Lower Umpqua and Siuslaw Indians conduct excavations at Camp Castaway, 2012. (Photo by the author.)

of the USCS. Excavations revealed much about this remarkable event in the history of early US presence on the Oregon coast (Figures 46–48). Tveskov has concluded that the site is indeed Camp Castaway. A large number of percussion caps suggest frequent firing of muskets at the site. This may reflect the reported use of gunshots in attempts to signal passing vessels offshore, or the shots may have been fired as a periodic display of weapons use when Native Americans were present. Musket balls are present at the site, both fired and unfired, but in much lower frequency than caps. It is unlikely that most of the gunfire involved rounds aimed at on-site targets. Abundant ship's hardware at the site may reveal patterns of tent construction, though dune shifts and other surface disturbance have likely redistributed many of these materials. As yet, no galley area has been identified, and there is relatively little archaeological data about the diet of site residents.

The Camp Castaway project demonstrates the archaeological value of USCS maps and field notes in combination with archaeological survey. The process of determining site or feature locations is not always direct, but USCS records are an invaluable data set for coastal archaeology. There are many West Coast sites yet to be identified using these methods.

Figure 46 Structural artifacts recovered during excavations at Camp Castaway. Top row: copper alloy nails and fragments of copper sheeting possibly from the hull of the *Captain Lincoln*. Bottom row: copper alloy ship spikes. These spikes are possibly structural elements from the ship from below the water line and were all recovered in the same immediate area of the site. Note the consistent angle of the shank, as if they were all torqued (and in one case, broken in half) in a similar manner when a portion of the ship was dismantled roughly. (Artifacts identified by Mark Tveskov and Chelsea Rose. Photo courtesy of Southern Oregon University Laboratory of Anthropology.)

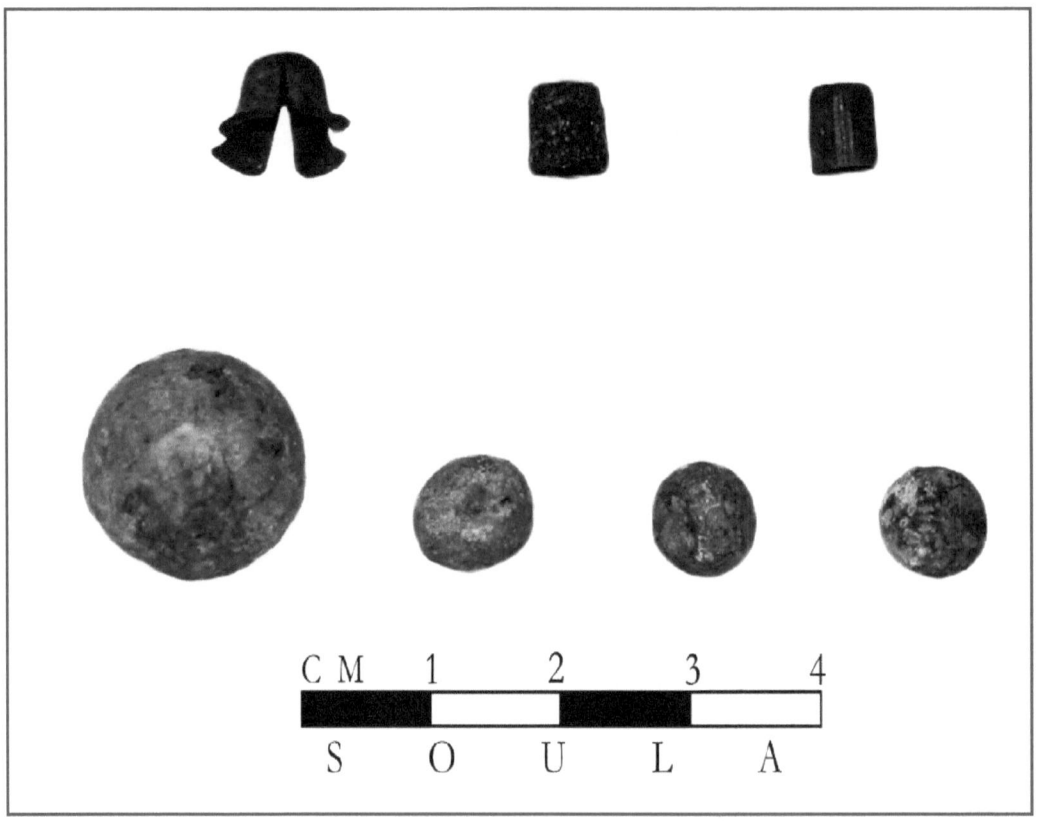

Figure 47 Pre–Civil War ammunition recovered during excavations at Camp Castaway. Top row: percussion caps from the Camp Castaway site. This artifact type was the most numerous diagnostic artifact at the site and was used in muzzle-loading long arms in the 1850s. The fired example (top left) is identical to many found at the Fort Lane site occupied by the US Army Dragoons during the same era. Bottom Row: a single .69-caliber and three .31-caliber musket balls. All four of these were found in the same shovelful of dirt at the Camp Castaway site. The model 1842 Springfield Musketoon was the standard long arm of the US Army Dragoons in the early 1850s, and their use by Company C, 1st Regiment of US Dragoons is attested to by the primary documents of the era and by the discovery of similar .69-caliber shot at the Fort Lane site. The Camp Castaway shot shown in this picture was likely from a single paper cartridge that was lost or discarded unfired, as a combination of a single .69-caliber ball with three .31-caliber balls was a popular way to load a musketoon by the Dragoons. (Artifacts identified by Mark Tveskov and Chelsea Rose. Photo courtesy of Southern Oregon University Laboratory of Anthropology.)

Figure 48 Domestic artifacts recovered during excavations at Camp Castaway. Top row: fragments of single dark olive glass bottle with a shallow kick-up, likely used for stout, ca. 1840s–1880s. Bottom row: fragments of a mid-nineteenth century, blue transfer print whiteware plate with a repeating floral motif on the rim and what might have been a romantic scene in the center. Neither the bottle nor the plate were standard military issue. (Artifacts identified by Mark Tveskov and Chelsea Rose. Photo courtesy of Southern Oregon University Laboratory of Anthropology.)

Chapter 6
Discussion and Conclusions

This volume presents examples of several USCS maps and survey station descriptions centering on the California coast. Most are only now being incorporated into archaeological research. The records examined here represent a small part of the USCS collection for the West Coast. From the first mapping in 1850 through George Davidson's departure in 1895, a remarkably detailed record was generated by USCS scientists. The full scope of its archaeological relevance is not known, yet based on the numerous examples presented here, some general assessments of the collection can be made.

The juxtaposition of period description and precision mapping in USCS scientific and cartographic records is the most remarkable aspect of this collection for archaeology. Situated description of historical structures, communities, activity areas, archaeological features, and other cultural phenomena at a given point in time is invaluable, particularly given the accuracy of USCS maps for many depicted locations. With this provenience information, significant reported sites can be relocated and their features delineated. Others previously unreported can now be identified. And new topics for coastal California archaeological research can be considered.

The Structure of USCS Research in Archaeology

There are many aspects of the USCS collection that are relevant for archaeological triangulation in California. The T-sheets and other maps represent sites in their settings at a specific point in time. Associated field notes depict earlier site history in some cases, and more often they relate aspects of site use at the time of the survey. The records illustrate many aspects of site setting and context, from tree cover and shoreline topography to road access and station intervisibility. When USCS records are related to other historic records, changes can be traced at nearly every documented site and its setting.

Perhaps the most dramatic aspect of the analysis of USCS records is what it reveals about new sites and site components. These records also provide detailed information about sites that were destroyed before they were recorded by archaeologists, such as the likely mounds at Seal Bluff and Little Coyote Point, Old Adobe at San Diego, Barry's Hotel at Sproul Plaza, and the shell mounds no longer present on San Nicolas Island and at Torrey Pines. There may be ongoing uncertainty as to the archaeological nature and origin of sites recorded by the USCS that are no longer extant, but other records can provide further support. For example, San Mateo Bridge engineering records may in the future clarify whether or not Little Coyote Point was composed of shell or other material. Similarly, land records may illuminate the antiquity of the residence at Old Adobe Station in San Diego.

In some cases the records provide several details about sites and features that inform archaeological interpretation. They present details of feature characteristics such as earthworks and adobe structure dimensions and configuration (El Castillo and Fort Mervine at Monterey, Ysidro Reyes adobe in Santa Monica, San Diego Old Adobe Station), mound topography (Shell Station at San Nicolas Island, CA-MRN-3 in Sausalito), and village layout (Tenas Illahee on the Columbia River and Ikso'ri at Humboldt Bay).

Many USCS maps, particularly T-sheets, portray integrated complexes of features that can be the basis for examining an archaeological landscape. The extent and relationship of various components can be assessed, and individual features can be viewed as part of a complex at locations such as the Call Ranch/Fort Ross area, the Richardson Rancho/MRN-3 mound at Sausalito, and several former mission communities in central and southern California.

Because USCS descriptions were intended for relocation of positions, the ethnicity of residents was sometimes a variable that surveyors used to distinguish a location in their notes and maps. Numerous station names include the word China or Chino, such as Chino Station (Figure 38) on San Nicolas Island and China Gulch near Point Sierra (Big Sur), and the Chinese fishing village at Point Molate was labeled as such. The Lowry Ranch was identified as "owned by a Negro man" in the description on Eimbeck's map. Numerous Native villages are identified as such. At the same time, distinct ethnic neighborhoods such as Native American villages near missions, the Chinese fishing community at Roseville, and the Portuguese whalers at Point San Luis were not identified by their ethnicity in USCS maps and notes.

Ethnic portrayals in USCS records can lead to new lines of inquiry on the diversity of West Coast heritage. Research on the Lowry Ranch helps to demonstrate that early African American homesteading and ranching in California was not limited to people who fled slavery and oppression in the South; there were also northeasterners who moved west to become ranchers. The records also show that Chinese fishing communities were widespread, possibly supporting the research of Bentz and Schwemmer (2002) and others who argue that fishing vessels arrived directly from China in the 1850s and that fishing wasn't simply an industry of former miners.

Detailed USCS portrayals of well-known sites are often more representative in terms of structure and infrastructure than other period records. The surveyors portrayed localities with the primary goal of relocating a survey marker, thus removing some types of bias from the representation.

There are also caveats in using USCS data. Analysis of specific locations using this data must address the sources of information available to the surveyor and potential biases or other filtering that may have conditioned their representations. While surveyors may have been more technically accurate in their depictions than travel writers or magazine artists in some respects, they were nonetheless selective about what they chose to depict in their sketches, maps, and notes. For example, communities that appeared transitory may have been left out in many cases, even if the presence of such communities was well established and seasonally repeated. Surveyors were often unfamiliar with local history, landowners, and place-names, so they frequently relied on local residents for this information, adding another layer of filtering to the data.

USCS records will increasingly play a role in clarifying the original location of sites that were reported but whose location is not otherwise confirmed or has been misplotted. For example, Nelson left no detailed map of the general setting of Bayshore Mound. Several episodes of archaeological probing in the area have identified site deposits, but some of these are clearly redeposited. Rodgers's map of the original shell mound location helps to clarify where at least some intact midden may be present beneath twentieth-century fill. These maps also provide the specificity needed to locate buried features that may be preserved in generally known locations, such as the Ysidro Reyes adobe and the Port Rumiantsev buildings. Named associations in very early records provide strong evidence of site use, as at the lone woman's cave on San Nicolas and the USS *Edith* wreck site, that might otherwise be identified as archaeological but not given a clear association.

Given the precision of USCS maps and published station coordinates, new findings from archival research can be corroborated through archaeological survey, as at Camp Castaway, or through additional archival research using other sources, such as homestead and census records relating to the Milford and Mary Jane Lowry ranch.

Changes to sites and their settings are illustrated in USCS records. Station maps, T-sheets, and field notes were often updated over time, so the changes undergone by a site can be examined by comparing different episodes of survey. For example, rapid erosion at Seal Bluff is documented from 1864 to 1878, and the complete loss of some shell mounds was observed by surveyors on San Nicolas Island between 1879 and 1908. These records portray the beginnings of some site components, such as Gold Rush–related industrial sites, while they show the ongoing and changing use of several longstanding features and site areas, such as villages, mounds, and presidios. They provide accurate, detailed information about site settings prior to extensive development, such as the marsh at Ellis Landing, the encinal at Oakland, US-period ranching and logging superimposed over the Russian site complex at Fort Ross, and some of the last views of earthworks before they were leveled by erosion and residential expansion. The records show that many Bay Area mound sites were used as landings in the mid- to late nineteenth century, which ironically may have preserved some of these sites when mounds were being looted and mound material was widely sought for road surfacing and farm soil enrichment. While most mound sites underwent rapid removal, such as the Torrey Pines mound, or burial by fill, such as Bayshore Mound, in some cases the USCS records show mounds and other sites undergoing gradual attrition from ongoing uses such as agriculture and recreational traffic (Burton Mound, Emeryville Shellmound) and town development (CA-MRN-3, West Berkeley).

Decline and revitalization of structures and site complexes is also rendered in drawings, maps, and notes. The architectural nadir of the Presidio was documented by Cutts in 1851. When compared with earlier Mexican- and Spanish-era maps and drawings as well as later renderings, the extent of structure loss prior to encapsulation of the officers' quarters is clear from the USCS map and drawing. In other cases the USCS mapped residences and settlements that were abandoned during or shortly after the Gold Rush, such as Governor

Burnett's house at Alviso, New Town at San Diego Bay and the short-lived structures of eastern Suisun Bay. Archaeological deposits associated with these settlements may be well preserved and potentially informative, as components may be largely discrete.

USCS records document at least two Native villages that were revitalized after undergoing periods of reduced population. The village of La Cieneguita at Mission Santa Barbara was shown as a ruin in 1853, yet this community continued to exist for decades after secularization (see Johnson 1995, Lightfoot 2005:218). At Tcet-xo village on the southern Oregon coast where settlers burned the Native American houses in 1853 (Douthit 2002), Chase's mapping data of 1870 shows that seven of the wooden houses had been rebuilt despite the growing presence of settlers in the area. The indigenous families there had developed a commercial fishery and a steam sawmill that also appears on the 1891 map.

New Research Directions

As USCS records add to the inventory of mounded sites, questions of mound distribution and interrelationships (Lightfoot 1997; Luby et al. 2006) can be further addressed. For example, Little Coyote Point is centrally located within southern San Francisco Bay, but its marsh setting suggests it was remote relative to terrestrial settings. If this was a large mound, it may have had a distinctive purpose related to its setting. Seal Bluff was somewhat closer to dry land, but it too may have had uses more oriented toward the open bay and surrounding wetlands. Freshwater may have been limited in each of these settings, except in winter when marsh pools such as the one mapped near Seal Bluff would have been less brackish. Studies of mound distribution on San Nicolas Island (Vellanoweth et al. 2002) can now be updated based on records of at least three mounds that were destroyed before being recorded by archaeologists in the mid-twentieth century.

Increasingly, accurate map data is being used in layered quantitative analysis in archaeology (Harris 2002). The USCS maps alone have value in portraying West Coast archaeological landscapes, but the descriptive text tied to these maps moves them into the realm of multi-layered data suited to GIS (Tripcevich and Byram 2013). Consider the Cutts map of the Santa Cruz primary triangulation station (Figure 28). Alone it offers information about the extent of structures and road networks in the hills north of Mission Santa Cruz in 1851–1852. Some structures appear as residences and others as barns or outbuildings. But the accompanying notes identify one large structure as Jordan's lime kiln. Given that Davis and Jordan are thought to have begun commercial lime production at this location in 1852, Cutts's map of the kiln is accurate enough to serve as a baseline rendering of this distinctive National Register–listed site prior to more extensive and better-documented lime production in the 1860s and 1870s. Given the detail in the Cutts map, the context of this Gold Rush–era industry can also be further explored.

USCS data are well suited to viewshed analysis in GIS. The intervisibility between survey positions was frequently addressed and documented by the surveyors. Because they often triangulated using shoreline mounds and other prominent sites as visual references, the intervisibility of mounds and other sites can be researched using USCS data.

USCS maps may be the earliest detailed records of several categories of linear sites, such as roads, fence lines, telegraph routes, flumes, and short-track rail lines. As map layers, linear sites illustrate the changing social and economic relationships within and between communities.

Short-lived settlements on transitory shorelines of the Sacramento River Delta region can be explored in detail, and new US-period sites can be brought into regional inventories despite the presence of levee fill or marsh subsidence. The USCS data also delineate long-term transitions from Native and Californio residences to Chinese fishing camps and early US ranches and farms.

As the abundant historical ecology data in the USCS records is further examined, following the work of the San Francisco Estuary Institute, it can provide important context for archaeological analysis. While not as accurate as aerial imagery, the T-sheets predate aerial imagery by 70 years for much of the coast. Tree cover is depicted in detail on many T-sheets, as this was a variable of much use to both surveyors and nearshore navigators. Shoreline wetland, beach, and dune settings are depicted with remarkable accuracy, and this may be of great relevance as wet-site archaeology continues to grow in the region.

Lightfoot et al. (2013) have demonstrated that the dimensions of size, structure, and landscape management practices are key to understanding the processes of cultural transformation for tribes in California beginning in the early colonial era. USCS maps and textual records hold much information relevant to the study of these communities from the mid-nineteenth century onward.

The Urgency of USCS Archival Analysis

Although the USCS records enhance our view of the archaeological record on the West Coast, they also demonstrate the rapid loss of archaeological features and in some cases entire sites over the past 162 years. Surveyors described some structures and earthworks as in ruins (Ysidro Reyes adobe), eroding and nearly lost (Seal Bluff, Old Adobe), likely to be destroyed (Little Coyote), and completely lost (San Nicolas Ridge and Slope mounds). As later records of the USCGS are further examined, information from return visits to many sites will likely reveal more examples of site deterioration documented by surveyors through the 1970s.

Despite cultural resource management legislation of the mid- to late twentieth century, many sites depicted by the USCS in the nineteenth century have been impacted or destroyed. When Pacific Gas and Electric began excavation for a planned nuclear plant construction at Bodega Head in the 1960s, archaeologists interested in the Russian port buildings at this location might have been able to conduct focused excavation or monitoring at the building sites had the 1862 and 1863 topographic maps of the area been available. In the 1990s the site of the Lowry Ranch became a landfill, and although the area was surveyed, no archaeological testing was done to determine whether buried features from this early ranch were present. The information about the Lowry family was not available using standard archival research techniques. Even in areas where some USCS research has been conducted by archaeologists and tribal cultural resource specialists, USCS records may still be left out of planning documents. On the south coast of Oregon in 2005, the North Bend Airport terminal was constructed at the location of one of the first USCS-identified shell mound and house pit sites at stations Pony and Violet (Lawson 1861), with no consideration of these records during Section 106 project planning.

Broader awareness of USCS records can now inform archaeological site management as well as academic research. The Seal Bluff site has been an area of fill deposition for decades, but reconstruction of the waterfront as well as subsurface soil treatment could lead to exposure of the site in the near future. Wetland and shoreline restoration at several other sites has the potential to expose previously unrecorded site deposits that can now be plotted using USCS records. Central Valley Flood Protection planning calls for levee changes that could affect Gold Rush–era sites mapped by the USCS in eastern Suisun Bay and the Sacramento River Delta. Multiple archaeological surveys have been conducted at Candlestick Point State Recreation Area and adjacent commercial property in the past decade under cultural resource regulations; future studies will now have access to the Rodgers (1894–1896) map of site CA-SFR-7. The numerous USCS-documented sites on state and federal lands along the central and southern California coast are gradually being added to inventories, with agencies such as the Channel Islands National Park conducting USCS records inventories (Byram 2012).

The USCS T-sheets are helping to clarify segmented linear sites on the north coast of California that are represented archaeologically. Linear sites and features present challenges for the researcher (Costello et al. 2007); disconnected segments may not be recognized as part of a single feature or network absent a detailed map from the era in which they were used. Sites such as log flumes in coastal forests are vulnerable to forest management practices and recreational road use if they are not documented. Map data also allow the extent of related feature complexes to be considered for integrated resource management.

While ship's hulls buried in bay mud at locations such as the San Francisco waterfront may be in anaerobic conditions suitable for long-term preservation (Delgado 2009), metal and wooden elements of shipwrecks in porous beach sand settings are more prone to oxidation and decomposition. This lends urgency to locating ships such as the schooner *Edith* in Santa Barbara County and the schooner *Captain Lincoln* near Coos Bay. The steam engine on the former is of particular importance due to its association with the designer Jon Ericsson. While wooden fish traps documented by the USCS in Oregon (Rockwell 1878) may be in less aerobic sediments, these archaeological features are known to be vulnerable to erosion in the seven Oregon estuaries where they have been identified (Byram 2002). Similar intertidal wooden features in Humboldt Bay or other California estuaries may be similarly vulnerable.

Triangulating Site Histories

In light of these findings of key archaeological data in USCS survey records, it seems appropriate to conclude this volume with a reconsideration of triangulation in archaeology. In qualitative social science research, triangulation is the process of addressing a research question or topic using more than two approaches, or the "method of cross-checking data from multiple sources to search for regularities in the research data" (O'Donoghue and Punch 2003:78). The approach can be applied in archaeology by drawing from multiple sources of data obtained with documented methods. Qualitative triangulation in cultural history has been discussed by Jarvis (2003:104). US Coast Survey maps and field notes represent a body of scientific research with historical and archaeological relevance that can be drawn from to triangulate the histories of archaeological landscapes.

Archaeology combines the qualitative and mathematical geographic aspects of triangulation. In field mapping, whether done by an archaeologist to establish a grid at a site or by a surveyor using a theodolite, measurement begins with a known baseline and extends geometrically across a series of planes. In this sense triangulation is the expansion of accurate position through line and angle measurement and use of mathematical theorems. Combining the qualitative and quantitative, USCS maps and situated description form a baseline for triangulating archaeological site histories. For much of the West Coast these are the first formal geographic records that are accurate enough to allow measurement of changes to archaeological landscapes over time. Although largely done outside formal archaeology, the nineteenth-century documents of the USCS on the West Coast set a baseline record for archaeological measurement and interpretation that began in the 1850s and encompassed several sites that were decades or centuries older.

Because of the early intensity of USCS mapping, these records can serve as baseline archaeological data for the early US-period on the California coast. From doghole ports like Fort Ross Cove to villages such as La Cieneguita, fortifications such as Presidio San Francisco to towns at landings such as Oakland and Old San Pedro, the settings of numerous archaeological landscapes were drawn with their more permanent structural or visual characteristics in mind. Mobile and more transitory phenomena are absent from these depictions, with exceptions such as Whistler's gulls in a small set of shoreline drawings, or the rare life sketch or ethnographic photo by Chase. While the landscapes have changed, the structures that were considered permanent enough to plot and render are most likely to represent predominant activities at a given location, and to correspond to archaeological features that can be identified today.

Appendix

California Topographic Sheets (T-sheets) ca. 1850–1895
in the Holdings of the Cartographic Records Division of the
National Archives and Records Administration II,
College Park, Maryland.

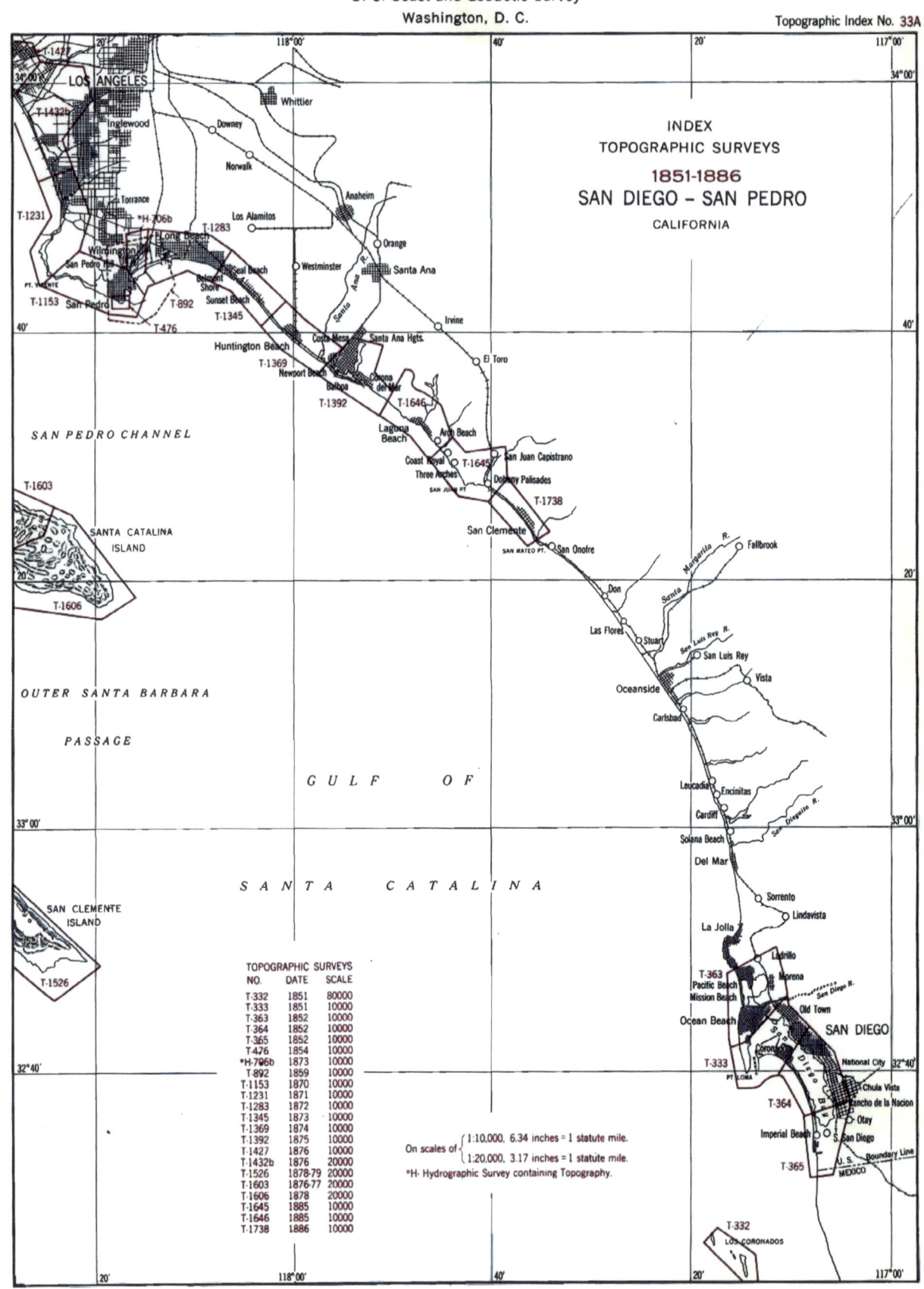

APPENDIX 85

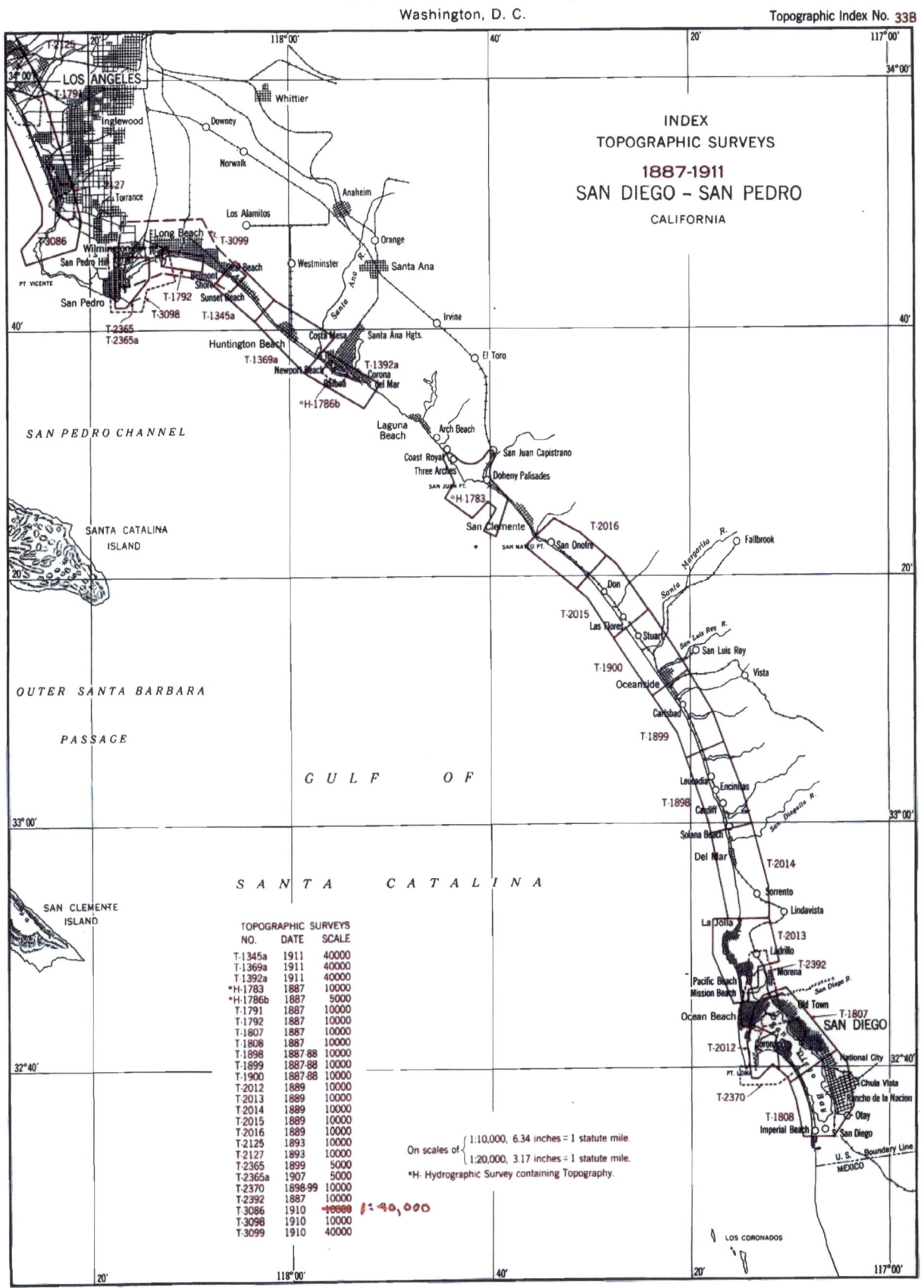

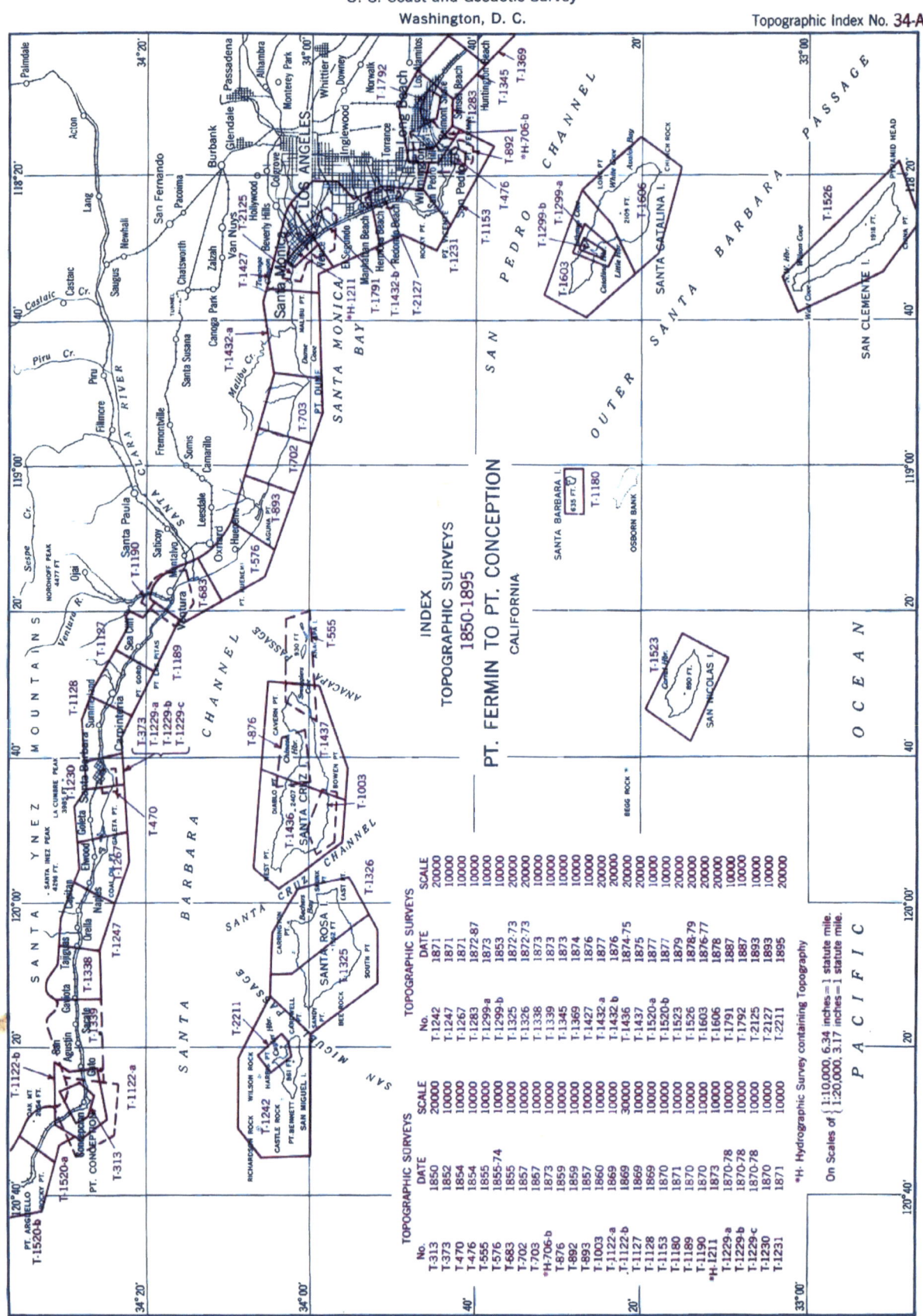

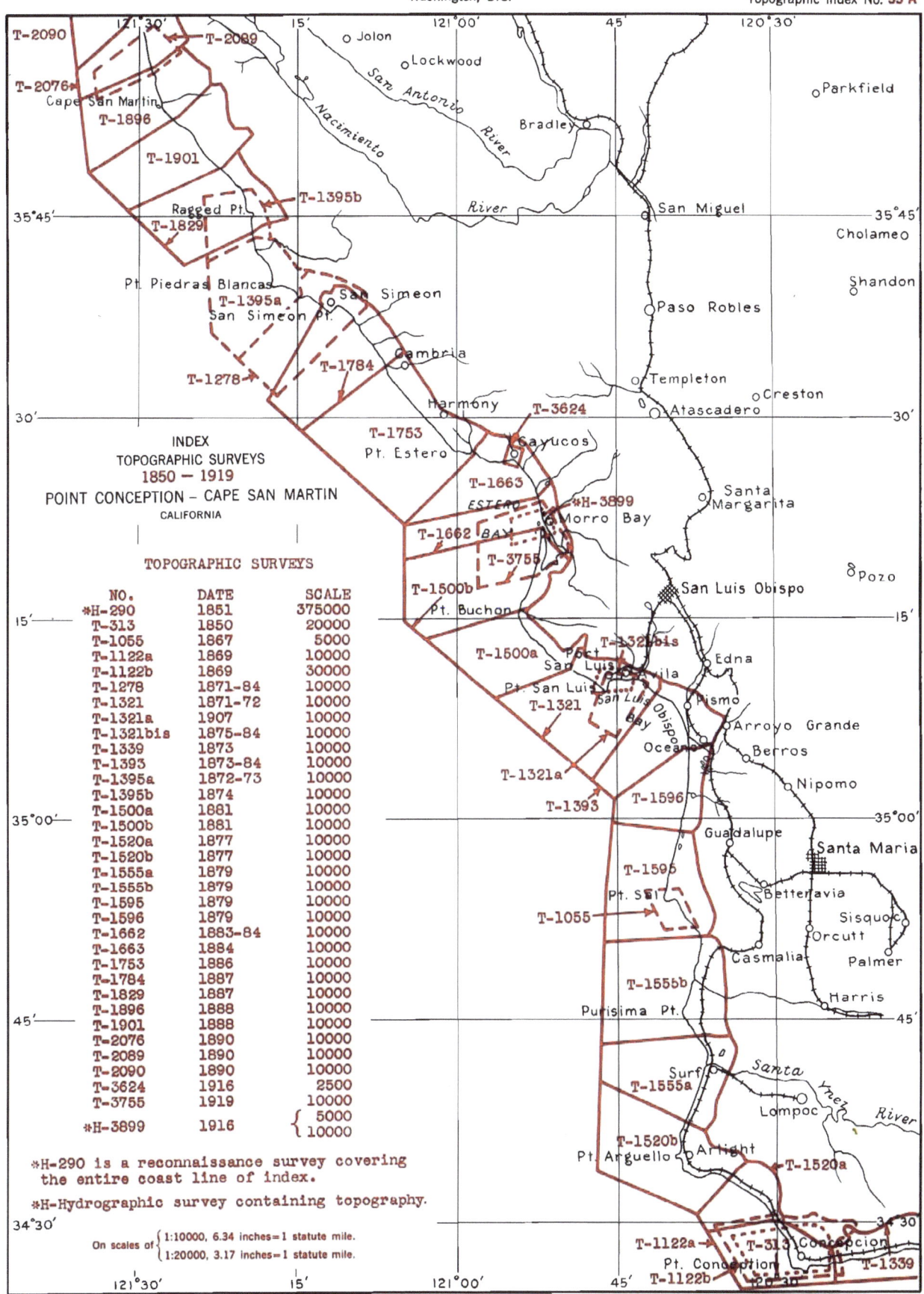

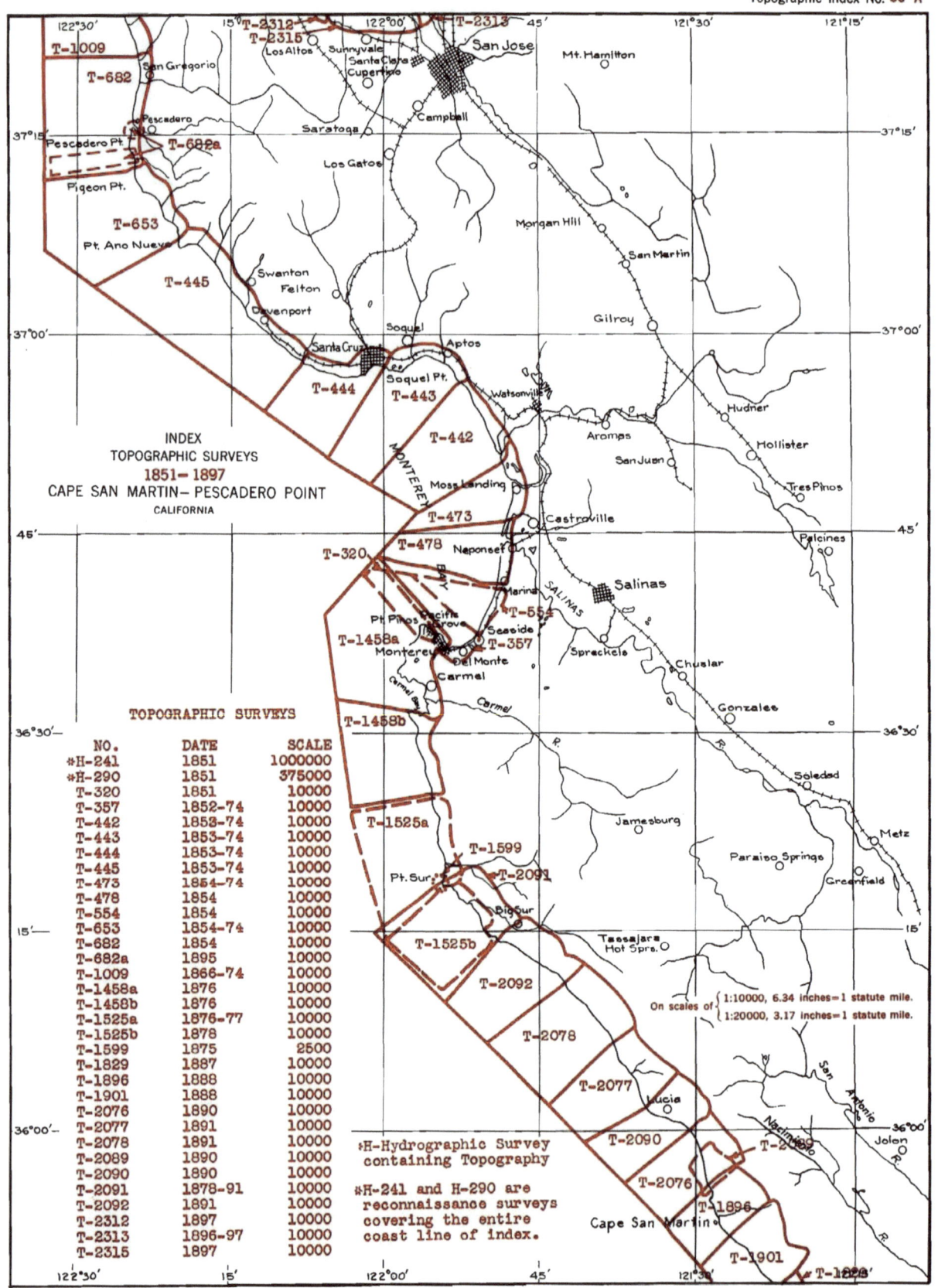

APPENDIX 89

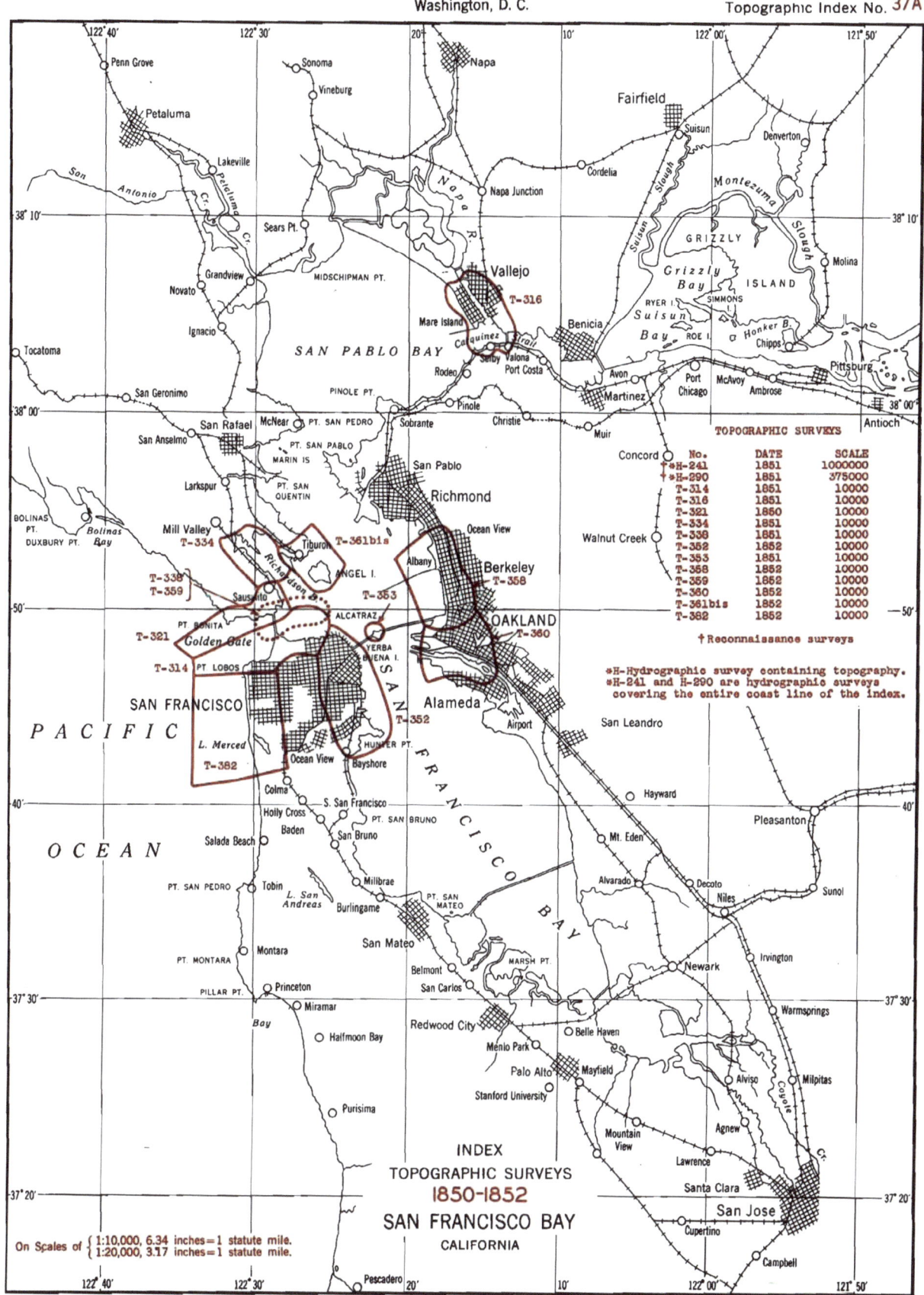

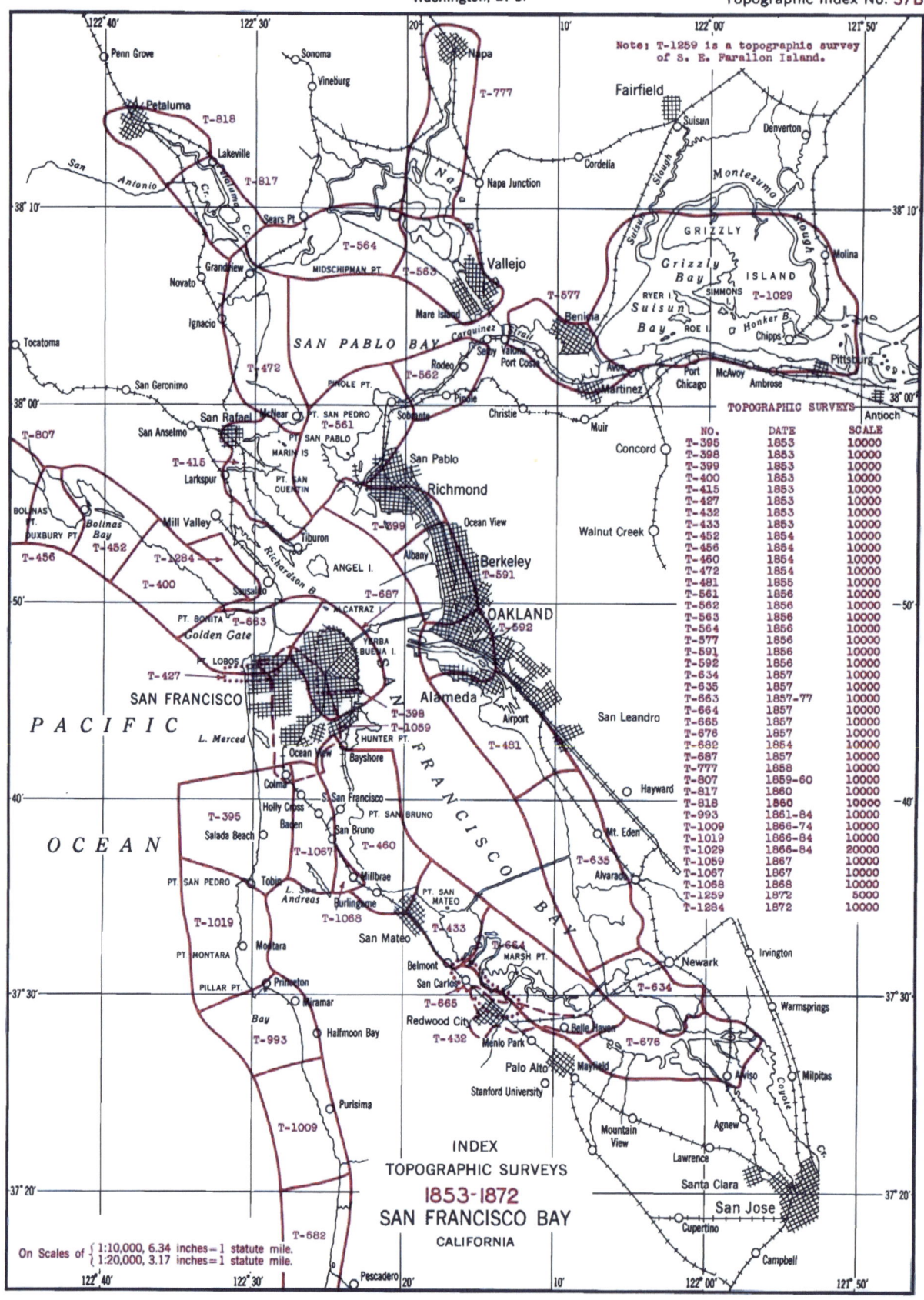

DEPARTMENT OF COMMERCE
U. S. Coast and Geodetic Survey
Washington, D. C.

Topographic Index No. 37C

TOPOGRAPHIC SURVEYS

NO.	DATE	SCALE
T-382a	1873	10000
T-1302	1873	10000
T-1302bis	1882	10000
T-1614	1881	10000
T-1616	1881	10000
T-1617	1881	10000
T-1618	1881-84	10000
T-1619	1882	10000
T-1620	1881	10000
T-1621	1881	10000
T-1622	1881	10000
T-1622b	1873	2000
T-1625	1881-82	10000
T-1625b	1884	10000
T-1629	1882	10000
T-1631	1882	10000
T-1632	1882	10000
T-1696	1886	10000
T-1697	1886	10000
⊕H-1785	1886-87	20000
T-1793	1886-87	10000
T-1803	1886	10000
T-1804	1887	10000
T-1825	1886	10000
T-1826	1886-87	10000
T-1827	1887	10000
T-1830	1887	10000
T-1831	1886	5000
T-1847	1887-88	10000
T-1848	1887	10000
T-2128	1887-92	10000

⊕H-1785 Hydrographic survey containing topography.

Note: T-1831 is a topographic survey of N. Farallon Island.

INDEX
TOPOGRAPHIC SURVEYS
1873-1887
SAN FRANCISCO BAY
CALIFORNIA

On Scales of { 1:10,000, 6.34 inches = 1 statute mile.
{ 1:20,000, 3.17 inches = 1 statute mile.

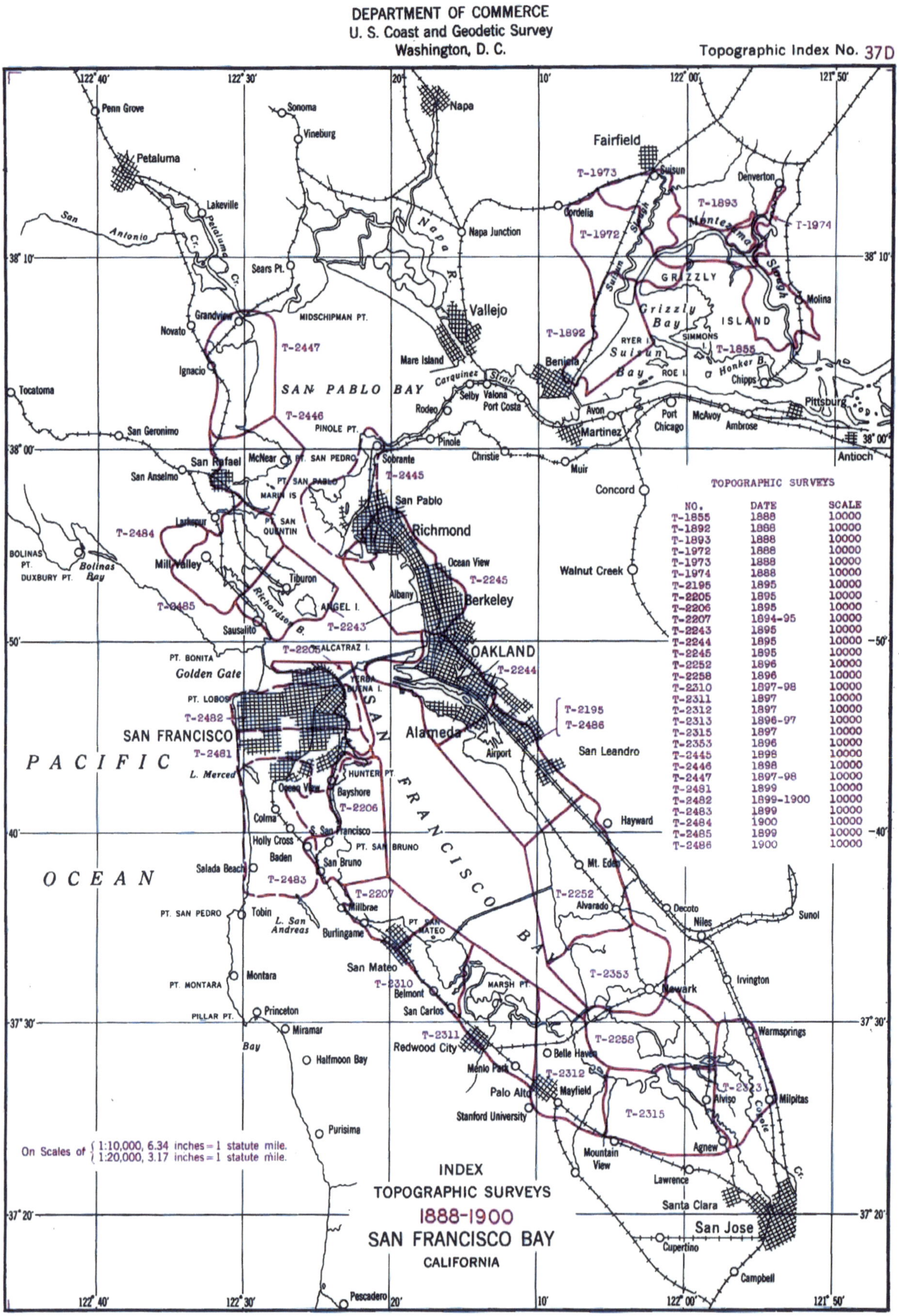
DEPARTMENT OF COMMERCE
U. S. Coast and Geodetic Survey
Washington, D. C.
Topographic Index No. 37D
TOPOGRAPHIC SURVEYS
NO. DATE SCALE
T-1855 1888 10000
T-1892 1888 10000
T-1893 1888 10000
T-1972 1888 10000
T-1973 1888 10000
T-1974 1888 10000
T-2195 1895 10000
T-2205 1895 10000
T-2206 1895 10000
T-2207 1894-95 10000
T-2243 1895 10000
T-2244 1895 10000
T-2245 1895 10000
T-2252 1896 10000
T-2258 1896 10000
T-2310 1897-98 10000
T-2311 1897 10000
T-2312 1897 10000
T-2313 1896-97 10000
T-2315 1897 10000
T-2353 1896 10000
T-2445 1898 10000
T-2446 1898 10000
T-2447 1897-98 10000
T-2481 1899 10000
T-2482 1899-1900 10000
T-2483 1899 10000
T-2484 1900 10000
T-2485 1899 10000
T-2486 1900 10000
On Scales of { 1:10,000, 6.34 inches = 1 statute mile. 1:20,000, 3.17 inches = 1 statute mile.
PACIFIC OCEAN
SAN PABLO BAY
SAN FRANCISCO BAY
SAN FRANCISCO
OAKLAND
INDEX
TOPOGRAPHIC SURVEYS
1888-1900
SAN FRANCISCO BAY
CALIFORNIA

APPENDIX

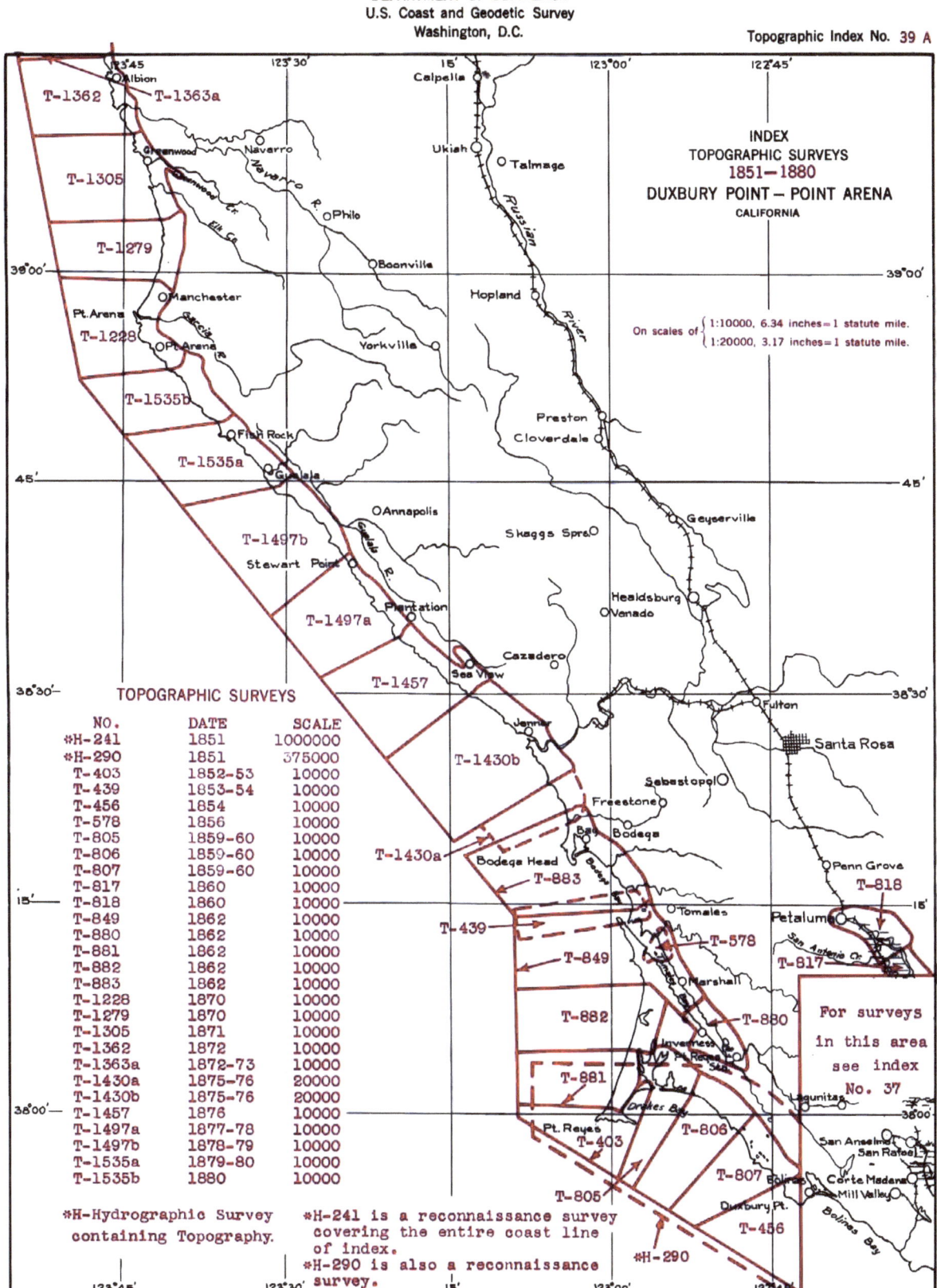

94　TRIANGULATING ARCHAEOLOGICAL LANDSCAPES

DEPARTMENT OF COMMERCE
U.S. Coast and Geodetic Survey
Washington, D.C.

Topographic Index No. 39 B

INDEX
TOPOGRAPHIC SURVEYS
1881–1931
DUXBURY POINT – POINT ARENA
CALIFORNIA

On scales of 1:10000, 6.34 inches = 1 statute mile.
1:20000, 3.17 inches = 1 statute mile.

TOPOGRAPHIC SURVEYS

NO.	DATE	SCALE
T-2977	1909	10000
T-2978	1909	10000
T-3840	1921	10000
T-4016	1922	10000
T-4208	1926	5000
T-4495	1929	10000
T-4501	1929	10000
T-4502	1929	10000
T-4503	1929	10000
T-4504	1929	10000
T-4505	1929	10000
T-4506	1929	10000
T-4507	1929	10000
T-4508	1929	10000
T-4517	1929	10000
T-4518	1929	10000
T-4519	1929	10000
T-4520	1929	10000
T-4593	1930	10000
T-4594	1930	5000 / 10000
T-4595	1930	10000
T-4596	1930	10000
T-4597	1930	10000
T-4637	1931	10000
T-4638	1931	10000
T-4639	1931	20000

For surveys in this area see index No. 37

APPENDIX 95

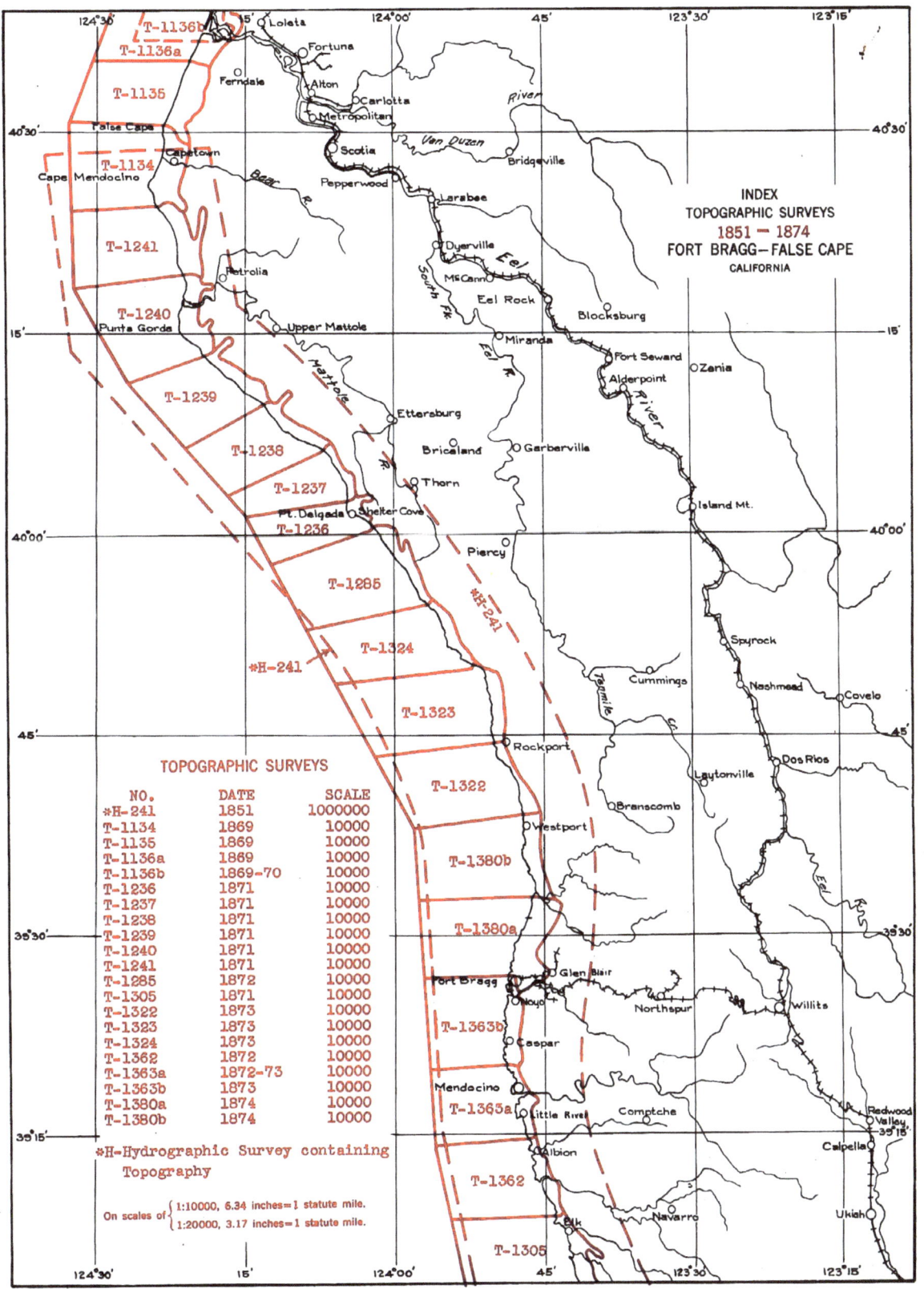

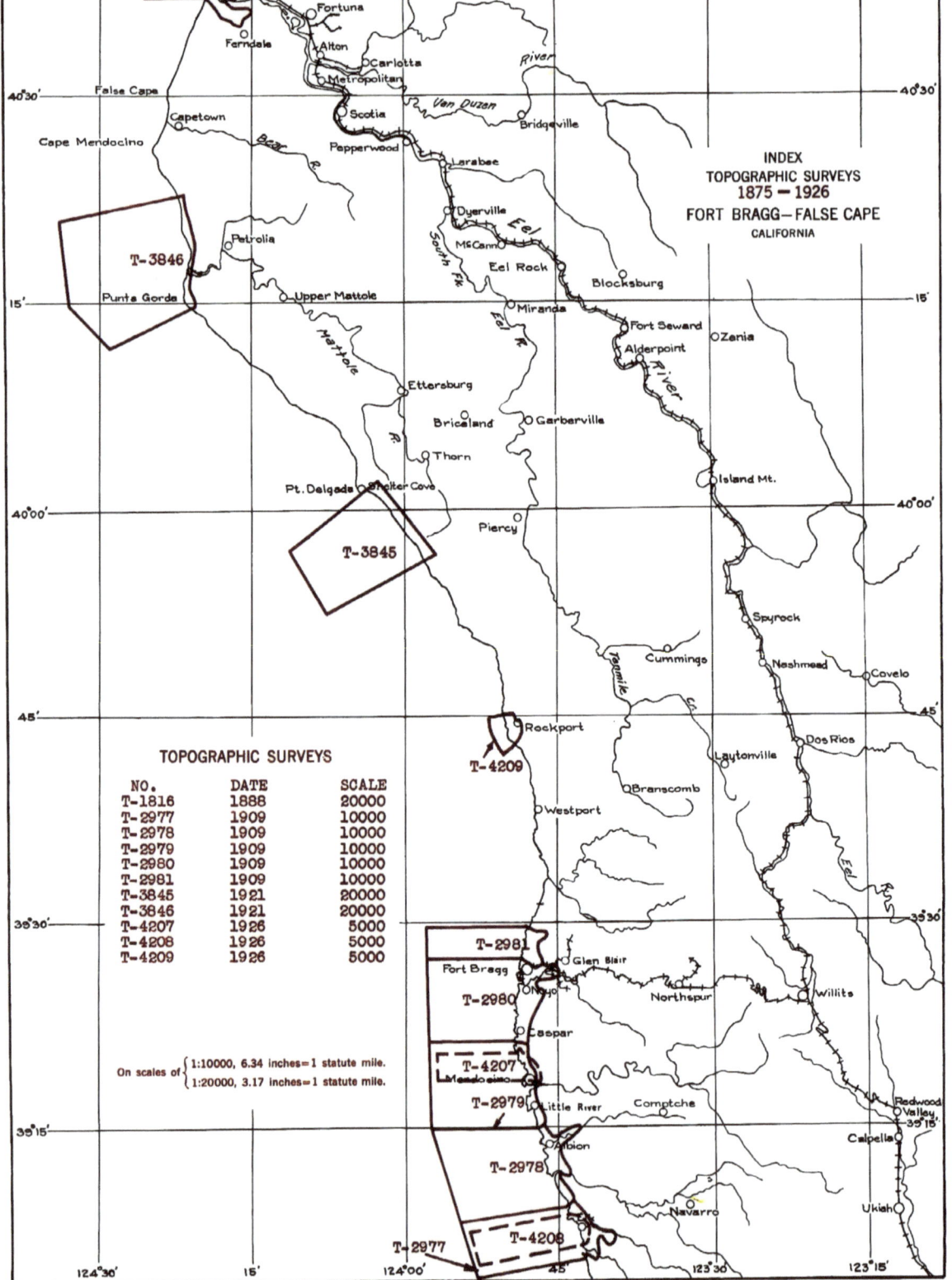

APPENDIX 97

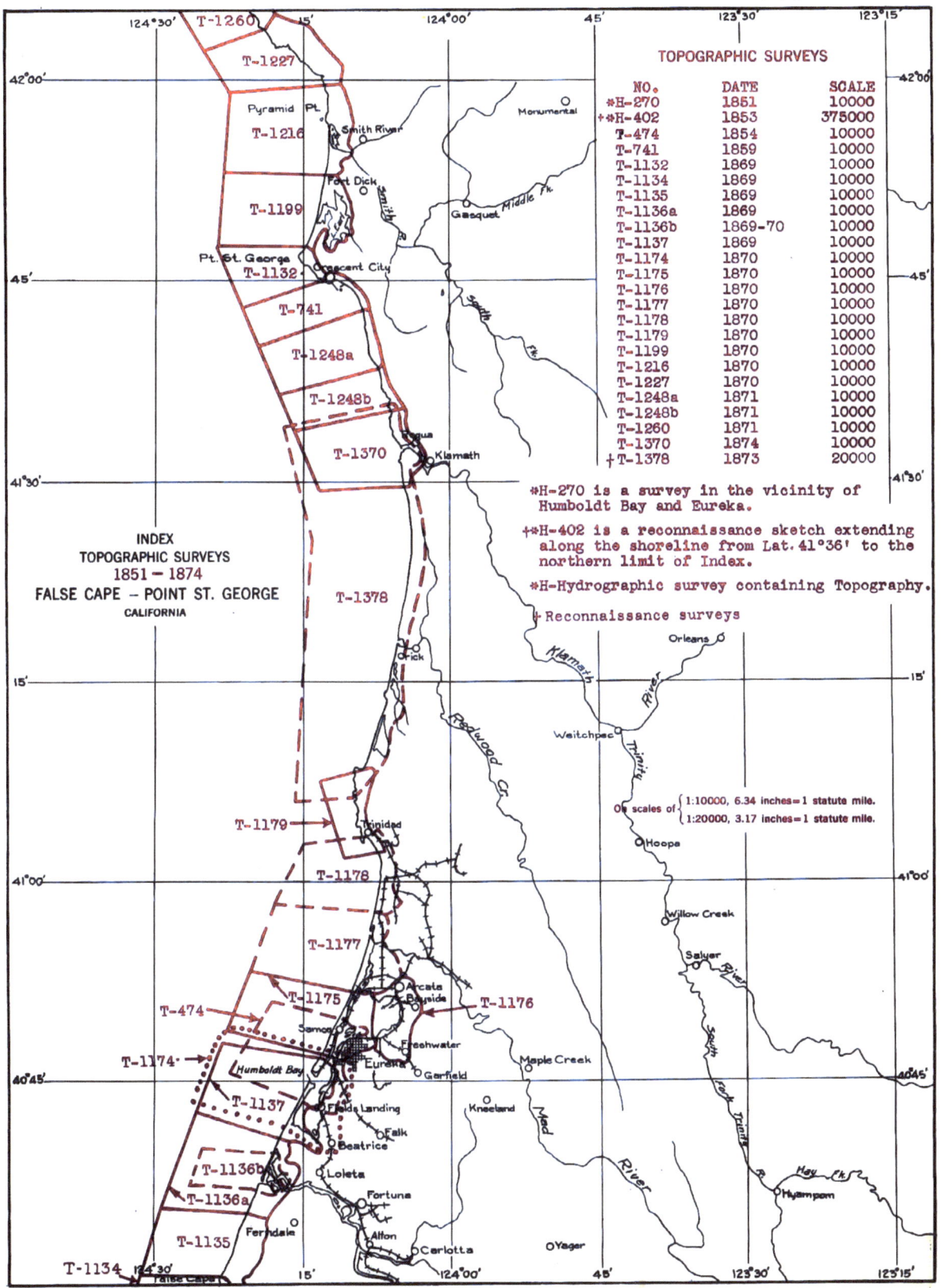

References

Alden, James
ca. 1851 Sketch Book of the S. Coast of California, Found in Archives at San Francisco by Geo. Davidson, 1888. GAR Series A G 11310, RG 23, National Archives and Records Administration II, College Park, MD.

Allen, John L.
1997 Imagining the West: The View from Monticello. In *Thomas Jefferson and the Changing West*, edited by James P. Ronda, pp. 3–23. University of New Mexico Press, Albuquerque.

Ambrose, Stephen
1962 *Halleck, Lincoln's Chief of Staff*. Louisiana State University Press, Baton Rouge.

Analytical Environmental Services
2009 Point Molate Mixed-Use Tribal Destination Resort and Casino Project Draft EIS/EIR. Report on file, City of Richmond Planning Department, Richmond, CA.

Bache, Alexander D.
1843–1865 Correspondence of A. D. Bache, Superintendent of the Coast and Geodetic Survey, 1843–1865. Microfilm M642, RG 23, National Archives and Records Administration II, College Park, MD.
1852 Report of the Superintendent of the Coast Survey. In *Annual Report of the Superintendent of the Coast Survey, Showing the Progress of that Work During the Year Ending November, 1851*, pp. 3–100. 32nd Congress, 1st Session, Robert Armstrong Printers, Washington, DC.

Baldwin, Albert L.
1904 Appendix 9: Triangulation in California, Part I. In *Report of the Superintendent of the Coast and Geodetic Survey, Showing the Progress of the Work from July 1, 1903, to June 30, 1904*, pp. 489–765. US Government Printing Office, Washington, DC.

Banks, Peter
1981 Subsurface Archaeological Investigations at CA-SFR-7, the Griffith-Shafter Mound and the Thomas Hawes Mound, along the Sunnydale-Yosemite Alignment 2A-1, San Francisco City and County, California. Report on file, Northwest Information Center, Rohnert Park, CA.

Barnard, F. A. P
1858 *Report on the History and Progress of the American Coast Survey up to the Year 1858*. American Association for the Advancement of Science, Washington, DC.

Bartel, Brad
1991 Archaeological Excavation and Education at the San Diego Royal Presidio, 1987–1990. Journal of San Diego History 37(1):28.

Beckham, Stephen D.
1974 National Register of Historic Places Eligibility Determination Record for Camp Castaway. Report on file, State Historic Preservation Office, Salem, OR.
2000 *Coos Bay North Spit: Historical Investigations of Federal Activities in Coastal Oregon.* Coos Bay Bureau of Land Management, North Bend, OR.

Bentz, Linda, and Robert Schwemmer
2002 The Rise and Fall of the Chinese Fisheries in California. In *The Chinese in America: A History from Gold Mountain to the New Millennium*, edited by Susie L. Cassel, pp. 140–155. AltaMira Press, Walnut Creek, CA.

Blackburn, Thomas C.
2005 Some Additional Alexander W. Chase Materials. *Journal of California and Great Basin Anthropology* 25(1):39–54.

Blank, Eugene L.
2009 Large California Tsunamis from Central Coast Historians and Central Coast Newspaper Records. Paper presented at the Fall 2009 meeting of the American Geophysical Union, San Francisco, Abstract #NH31B-1113.

Bradford, George
1878–1879 Descriptions of Stations, Suisun Bay and San Pablo. GA Series 31653, RG 23, National Archives and Records Administration II, College Park, MD.

Byram, R. Scott
2002 Brush Fences and Basket Traps: The Archaeology and Ethnohistory of Tidewater Weir Fishing on the Oregon Coast. Unpublished Ph.D. dissertation, Department of Anthropology, University of Oregon, Eugene.
2005 The Work of a Nation: Richard D. Cutts and the US Coast Survey Map of Fort Clatsop. *Oregon Historical Quarterly* 106(2):254–271.
2006 SHPO Site Record for 35CS221. Report on file, State Historic Preservation Office, Salem, OR.
2009a Chetco Indian Memorial Planning. Letter report on file, Confederated Tribes of Siletz Indians, Siletz, OR.
2009b Shell Mounds and Shell Roads: The Destruction of Oregon Coast Middens for Early Road Surfacing. *Current Archaeological Happenings in Oregon* 34(1):6–14.
2011 Letter to Sandra Stephens, EHP Specialist, re: FEMA 1964-DR-OR Port of Brookings tsunami damage emergency construction. Manuscript on file, Federal Emergency Management Offices, Portland, OR.
2012 US Coast Survey Maps and Field Notes for Santa Rosa Island. Report on file, Channel Islands National Park, Ventura, CA.

California Academy of Sciences (CAS)
1873 *Proceedings of the California Academy of Sciences*, Series 1, Vol. 4, 1868–1872. San Francisco.

California Department of Boating and Waterways and State Coastal Conservancy (CADBWSCC)
2002   California Beach Restoration Study, http://www.dbw.ca.gov/PDF/Reports/BeachReport/Ch8_Bluffs.pdf, accessed December 2012.

California Department of Parks and Recreation
2004   Final Mitigation Negative Declaration. Fort Ross State Historic Park Water Supply System Improvements Project SCH #2004012100. Report on file at the Department of Parks and Recreation, Sacramento.

Chase, Alexander W.
1869a   Siletz, or "Lo" Reconstructed. *Overland Monthly* 2(5):424–434.
1869b   Descriptions of Stations, Point St. George and Crescent City Reef. GA Series 2073, RG 23, National Archives and Records Administration II, College Park, MD.
1872   Descriptions of Stations, East of San Pedro Bay (duplicate). GA Series 2089, RG 23, National Archives and Records Administration II, College Park, MD.
1872–1873 Description of Stations, South of False Klamath and South of Klamath River. GA Series, RG 23, National Archives and Records Administration II, College Park, MD.
1873   Descriptions of Stations, East of San Pedro near Anaheim Landings, California. GA Series GA-2094, RG 23, National Archives and Records Administration II, College Park, MD.
1875   Descriptions of Stations, Vicinity of Santa Monica, Los Angeles County, California. GA Series 2101, RG 23, National Archives and Records Administration II, College Park, MD.

Chavez, David, and John Holson
1985   Cultural/Archaeological Resources Investigation at the Naval Supply Center Fuel Department, Point Molate, Contra Costa County, California. Report on file, Northwest Information Center, Rohnert Park, CA.

Cloud, John
2007   George Davidson and the Point of Beginning. *Coast and Ocean* 33(2), http://coastandocean.org/coast_v23_no2_2007/articles/cloud_03.htm, accessed October 2012.
2008   E-mail to Scott Byram, January 3, 2008.
2013   A Field Guide to the Coast Survey in 19th-Century California. Paper presented at the 47th Annual Meeting of the Society for California Archaeology, Berkeley, CA.

Collier, Mary E. T., and Sylvia B. Thalman
1996   *Interviews with Tom Smith and Maria Copa: Isabel Kelley's Ethnographic Notes on the Coast Miwok Indians of Marin and Southern Sonoma Counties, California*. Occasional Paper No. 6. Miwok Archaeological Preserve of Marin, San Rafael, CA.

Colonna, Benjamin A.
1878   Primary Triangulation North of San Francisco. GA Series 31471, RG 23, National Archives and Records Administration II, College Park, MD.
1880a   Nine Days on the Summit of Mt. Shasta, http://www.lib.noaa.gov/edocs/shasta.html, accessed February 2011.
1880b   Descriptions of Stations, Main Triangulation, Sacramento and San Joaquin Valleys. GA Series 34991 or 34491 (conflicting records), RG 23, National Archives and Records Administration II, College Park, MD.

Contra Costa County
2007   Mount Diablo Creek Watershed Plan (Draft). Document on file, County Records Office, Martinez, CA.

Costello, Julia G., Rand F. Herbert, and Mark D. Selverston
2007   Mining Sites: Historic Context and Archaeological Research Design, http://www.sonoma.edu/asc/publications/hard/mining%20research%20design_draft2_web.pdf, accessed March 2012.

Cutts, Richard D.
1851–1852 Descriptions of Stations, Primary Triangulation between San Francisco and Monterrey Bay. GA Series 24610, RG 23, National Archives and Records Administration II, College Park, MD.
1853a   Appendix 29: Extracts from a Letter of Richard D. Cutts Esq., Assistant U.S. Coast Survey to the Superintendent, dated April 4, 1852. In *Report of the Superintendent of the Coast Survey, Showing the Progress of the Survey during the Year 1852,* pp. 129–130. 32nd Congress, 2nd Session, House Executive Document No. 58. Robert Armstrong Public Printer, Washington, DC.
1853b   Appendix 25: Correspondence of Assistant R. D. Cutts with the Secretary of the Commission for Locating the Naval Depot at San Francisco. In *Report of the Superintendent of the Coast Survey, Showing the Progress of the Survey during the Year 1852,* pp. 123–124. 32nd Congress, 2nd Session, Executive No. 58. Robert Armstrong Public Printer, Washington, DC.
1871   Appendix 7: Memoranda Relating to the Field-work of Secondary Triangulation. In *Annual Report of the Superintendent of the US Coast Survey, Showing the Progress of the Survey during the Year 1868*, pp. 109–139. 40th Congress, 3rd Session, House Executive Document No. 71. US Government Printing Office, Washington, DC.
1878   *General Instructions Hydrographic Surveys Division in Regard to Inshore Hydrographic Work of the Coast Survey, 1878.* US Government Printing Office, Washington, DC.

Daily Alta California
1852   Wreck of the Oxford. July 17. San Francisco.

Daniel, Thomas F.
2008   One Hundred and Fifty Years of Botany at the California Academy of Sciences (1853–2003). *Proceedings of the California Academy of Sciences*, Series 4, 59(7):215–305. San Francisco.

Davidson, George
1858   *Directory for the Pacific Coast of the United States.* US Government Printing Office, Washington, DC.
1860   Additional Descriptions of Stations, Primary Triangulation North of San Francisco. GA Series 26489, RG 23, National Archives and Records Administration II, College Park, MD.
1871   Descriptions of Stations, San Diego Bay, California (with tracing of 1859 T-sheet). GA Series 4532, RG 23, National Archives and Records Administration II, College Park, MD.

Davidson, George (continued)
1887   Appendix 7: Report for 1886. In *Methods and Results: Voyages of Discovery and Exploration on the Northwest Coast of America from 1539 to 1603*, edited by George Davidson, pp. 155–253. US Coast and Geodetic Survey, Washington, DC.
1889   *US Coast and Geodetic Survey Pacific Coast Pilot of California, Oregon, and Washington*. 4th edition. US Government Printing Office, Washington, DC.

de Cessac, Jean F. A. L.
1951   L. de Cessac's Report on His Activities in California. In The French Scientific Expedition to California, 1877–1879, edited by Robert F. Heizer. *Reports of the University of California Archaeological Survey* 12:8–13.

Delgado, James P.
2009   *Gold Rush Port: The Maritime Archaeology of San Francisco's Waterfront*. University of California Press, Berkeley.

Dibblee, Thomas W.
1981   *Preliminary Geologic Map of the Port Chicago Quadrangle, Contra Costa County, California*. US Geological Survey, Open-file Report 81-101. Scale 1:24,000.

Dicken, Samuel
1961   *Pioneer Trails of the Oregon Coast*. University of Oregon Press, Eugene.

Dickens, Edmund F.
1889   Descriptions of Stations, Coos Bay, Oregon. GA Series 13090, RG 23, National Archives and Records Administration II, College Park, MD.

Dickie, George W., Ralph Harrison, and Samuel B. Christy
1914   George Davidson. *Proceedings of the California Academy of Sciences*, Series 4, Vol. 4:10–13. San Francisco.

Dodge, Orvil
1898   *Pioneer History of Coos and Curry Counties, Oregon*. Capital Printing Company, Salem.

Douthit, Nathan
2002   *Uncertain Encounters: Indians and Whites at Peace and War in Southern Oregon, 1820s–1860s*. Oregon State University Press, Corvallis.

Dracup, Joseph
2006   Geodetic Surveys in the United States: The Beginning and the Next One Hundred Years, http://www.history.noaa.gov/stories_tales/geodetic3.html, accessed March 2012.

Duncan-Abrams, Marguerite, and Barbara Milkovich
1995   *City of Redondo Beach Historic Context Statement*, Historical Resources Management. Report on file, City of Redondo Beach Planning Department, Redondo Beach, CA.

Duvall, Charles R., and Albert L. Baldwin
1911 Appendix 5: Triangulation of California, Part II. In *Report of the Superintendent of the USCGS Showing the Progress of the Work from July 1, 1909–July 1, 1910*, pp. 173–430. US Government Printing Office, Washington, DC.

Eimbeck, William
1876 Descriptions of Stations, Across California (duplicate). GA Series 2104, RG 23, National Archives and Records Administration II, College Park, MD.

Eldredge, Zoeth S.
1915 *History of California*, Vol. 5. The Century History Company, New York.

Engstrom, Wayne N.
2006 Nineteenth Century Coastal Geomorphology of Southern California. *Journal of Coastal Research* 224:847–861.

Fairfield, George A.
1855–1858 Descriptions of Stations, Tomales Bay and Petaluma Creek. GA Series 25466, RG 23, National Archives and Records Administration II, College Park, MD.

Fairfield, William
1907 Descriptions of Stations, Pulgas Base Line and Vicinity. GA Series 60541, RG 23, National Archives and Records Administration II, College Park, MD.

Forney, Stehman
1872 T-sheet 1326, Santa Rosa Island, California. Cartographic Records, RG 23, National Archives and Records Administration II, College Park, MD.
1879 Descriptions of Stations, San Nicholas Island, California. GA Series F2111, RG 23, National Archives and Records Administration II, College Park, MD.

Gamble, Lynn H.
2011 *The Chumash World at European Contact: Power, Trade, and Feasting Among Complex Hunter-Gatherers.* University of California Press, Berkeley.

Garcia, Tracy
2010 Colonial Encounters with the Past: Paul Schumacher, the Smithsonian Institution, and the Origins of Pacific Coast Archaeology. Unpublished Master's thesis, Department of Anthropology, University of Oregon, Eugene.

Goerke, Betty
2007 *Chief Marin: Leader, Rebel and Legend.* Heyday Books, Berkeley, CA.

Goodman, Dean
2009 Pascual Marquez Family Cemetery in Rancho Boca de Santa Monica. Ground penetrating radar report, La Señora Research Institute, Santa Barbara, http://www.gpr-survey.com/gprslice2/cemeteries.html, accessed October 2012.

Greenwell, William E.
1853–1856 Signal Book of Secondary Triangulation in the Vicinity of San Pedro. GA Series, RG 23, National Archives and Records Administration II, College Park, MD.
1855–1860 Descriptions of Stations, Santa Barbara Channel. GA-25716, RG 23, National Archives and Records Administration II, College Park, MD.
1856–1857 Descriptions of Signals, Santa Cruz Island (duplicate). GA Series 13070, RG 23, National Archives and Records Administration II, College Park, MD.
1862–1863 "Vicinity of Santa Barbara East and West," in Descriptions of Stations, Santa Barbara Channel and Vicinity, by George Davidson, Edward O. C. Ord, W. E. Greenwell and D. Delehanty. GA Series 25047, RG 23, National Archives and Records Administration II, College Park, MD.
1866 Descriptions of Stations, Suisun Bay. GA Series 24610, RG 23, National Archives and Records Administration II, College Park, MD.
1878 Descriptions of Stations, Promontory Point to Point Sal. GA Series 31684-A, RG 23, National Archives and Records Administration II, College Park, MD.

Grossinger, Robin, Eric Stein, Kristen Cayce, Shawna Dark, Ruth Askevold, and Alison Whipple
2011 Historical Wetlands of the Southern California Coast: An Atlas of US Coast Survey T-sheets, 1851–1889. San Francisco Estuary Institute, Richmond, CA.

Gudde, Erwin G.
1951 Mutiny on the Ewing. *The Journal*, US Coast and Geodetic Survey, No. 4, December 1951, http://www.history.noaa.gov/stories_tales/ewingmutiny.html, accessed November 2012.

Haraszthy, Agostin
1859 Report on Grapes and Wines of California. *Transactions of the California State Agricultural Society*, 1858. Appendix Vol. 6, pp. 311–329 in 10th Session, California State Senate Reports. John O'Meara, State Printer, Sacramento.

Harris, Trevor M.
2002 GIS in Archaeology. In *Past Time, Past Place: GIS for History*, edited by Anne K. Knowles, pp. 131–143. ESRI Press, Redlands, CA.

Harrison, Alexander M.
1851 Sketch J No. 4 Indicating Proposed Sites for a Light-House on Point Pinos, Bay of Monterey, http://www.photolib.noaa.gov/htmls/cgs05104.htm, accessed December 2012.
1853 Preliminary Sketch of Santa Barbara California. Engraving attached to Description of Signals, Santa Barbara Channel Primary Triangulation 1855–1860, by W. E. Greenwell. GA Series 25716, RG 23, National Archives and Records Administration II, College Park, MD.
1867 Appendix 22: On the Plane-Table and Its Use in Topographical Surveying. In *Annual Report of the Superintendent of the US Coast Survey Showing the Progress for the Year 1865*, pp. 203–231. US Government Printing Office, Washington, DC.

Haugan, Jevne
2005 Dog Holes and Wire Chutes: From Sailing to Steaming in the Lumber Trade. *Maritime Life and Traditions* 29:20–25.

Hayes, Derek
2007 *Historical Atlas of California*. University of California Press, Berkeley.

Hayford, John F., and Albert L. Baldwin
1908 *The Earth Movements in the California Earthquake of 1906*. US Coast and Geodetic Survey. US Government Printing Office, Washington, DC.

Heizer, Robert F.
1978 Introduction. In *California*, edited by Robert Heizer and William C. Sturtevant, pp. 1–5. Handbook of North American Indians, Vol. 8, William C. Sturtevant, general editor. Smithsonian Institution, Washington, DC.

Hergesheimer, Edwin
1881 Appendix 11: Methods and Results, Report on the Preparation of Standard Topographical Drawings. In *Annual Report for 1879*, US Coast and Geodetic Survey, p. 191. US Government Printing Office, Washington, DC.

Holland, Katherine C.
1997 James Madison Alden Watercolors and Drawings. Exhibition of the California Historical Society, http://www.californiahistoricalsociety.org/exhibits/past_exhibits/james_alden/index.html#, accessed January 2012.

Hudson, Travis
1981 Recently Discovered Accounts Concerning the "Lone Woman" of San Nicolas Island. *Journal of California and Great Basin Anthropology* 3(2):187–199.

Hughes, Edan
2002 *Artists in California, 1786–1940*. Crocker Art Museum, Sacramento, CA.

Huston, Alan F.
2000 Cadwalader Ringgold, US Navy: Gold Rush Surveyor of San Francisco Bay and Waters to Sacramento, 1849–1850. *California History* 79(4):208–221.

Jarvis, William E.
2003 *Time Capsules: A Cultural History*. McFarland and Co., Jefferson, NC.

Jefferson, Thomas
1955 *Notes on the State of Virginia*. Edited by William Peden. University of North Carolina Press, Chapel Hill.

Johnson, John R.
1995 *The Chumash Indians After Secularization*. California Mission Studies Association, Bakersfield.

Keller, Edward A., and Larry D. Gurolla
2000 *Final Report, July 2000, Earthquake Hazard of the Santa Barbara Fold Belt, California*. Institute for Crustal Studies, University of California, Santa Barbara.

Kentta, Robert
2011   Transcriptions of the journals of A. W. Chase. Manuscript on file, Confederated Tribes of Siletz Indians, Siletz, OR.

Kirkman, George W.
1937   Pictorial and Historical Map of Los Angeles County. Map on file, Los Angeles Public Library, Los Angeles, CA.

Komar, Paul D.
1997   *The Pacific Northwest Coast: Living with the Shores of Oregon and Washington*. Duke University Press, Durham, NC.

Lareau, S. D.
1984   Station Recovery, Loon EW3874. National Ocean Service Triangulation Record. Report on file, NOAA Central Library, Silver Spring, MD.

Lawson, James
1861   Descriptions of Stations, Coose Bay, Oregon. GA Series 26638, RG 23, National Archives and Records Administration II, College Park, MD.
1864   Descriptions of Stations, Suisun Bay (duplicate). GA Series 26494, RG 23, National Archives and Records Administration II, College Park, MD.
ca. 1880 Autobiography. US Coast and Geodetic Survey documents, http://www.history.noaa.gov/stories_tales/jlawson.html, accessed March 2012.

Lee, Murray
2010   *In Search of Gold Mountain: A History of the Chinese in San Diego*. Donning Company Publishers, Virginia Beach, VA.

Lewis, Oscar
1954   *George Davidson: Pioneer West Coast Scientist*. University of California Press, Berkeley.

Lightfoot, Kent G.
1997   Cultural Construction of Coastal Landscapes: A Middle Holocene Perspective from the San Francisco Bay. In *Archaeology of the California Coast During the Middle Holocene*, edited by Jon M. Erlandson and Michael Glassow, pp. 129–141. Institute of Archaeology, University of California, Los Angeles.
2005   *Indians, Missionaries, and Merchants: The Legacy of Colonial Encounters on the California Frontiers*. University of California Press, Berkeley.

Lightfoot, Kent G., Lee M. Panich, Tsim D. Schneider, Sara L. Gonzalez, Matthew A. Russell, Darren Modzelewski, Theresa Molino, and Elliot H. Blair
2013   The Study of Indigenous Political Economies and Colonialism in Native California: Implications for Contemporary Tribal Groups and Federal Recognition. *American Antiquity* 78(1):89–104.

Livingston, Dewey
2004   *National Park Service Cultural Landscapes Survey, Santa Cruz Island Ranching District*. Report on file, Channel Islands National Park, Ventura, CA.

Los Angeles Herald
1875 Exports and Imports at Anaheim Landing. January 12, Vol. 3(89):3, col. 4.

Loud, Llewellyn L.
1918 *Ethnography and Archaeology of the Wiyot Territory*. University of California Publications in American Archaeology and Ethnology 14(3). Berkeley, CA.

Luby, Edward M., Clayton D. Drescher, and Kent G. Lightfoot
2006 Shell Mounds and Mounded Landscapes in the San Francisco Bay Area: An Integrated Approach. *Journal of Island and Coastal Archaeology* 1:191–214.

Lyman, Albert
1851 Journal of Captain Albert Lyman, entry for Oct. 29, 1851. Manuscript on file, Douglas County Museum, Roseburg, Oregon.

Lyman, R. Lee
1991 Alexander W. Chase and the Nineteenth-Century Archaeology and Ethnography of the Southern Oregon and Northern California Coast. *Northwest Anthropological Research Notes* 25(2):155–256.

MacMullen, Jerry
1962 The Presidio of San Diego. *Journal of San Diego History* 8(2):21.

Maher, Thomas J.
1933 *The Coast Survey on the Pacific Coast.* US Coast and Geodetic Survey, http://www.history.noaa.gov/stories_tales/pacifichistory.html, accessed December 2012.

Marquez, Ernest
2011 *Santa Monica Beach: A Collector's Pictorial History*. Angel City Press, Los Angeles.

Martz, Patricia
2008 *4000 Tears on GHALAS-AT: Part One of the San Nicolas Island Index Unit Analysis Program*. Report prepared for Naval Air Weapons Station, China Lake, on file at the Department of Anthropology, California State University, Los Angeles.

Matchette, Robert B.
1995 *Guide to Federal Records in the National Archives of the United States.* 3 vols. National Archives and Records Administration, Washington, DC. Online at http://www.archives.gov/research/guide-fed-records/groups/023.html#23.4.2.

May, Ronald V.
1985 Schooners, Sloops and Ancient Mariners: Research Implications of Shore Whaling in San Diego. *Pacific Coast Archaeological Society Quarterly* 21(4):1–24. Pacific Coast Archaeological Society, Costa Mesa.
1995 Evidence for the Physical Appearance of 18th Century Spanish Cannon Batteries in California. *Fort Guijarros Journal* 1:4–15. Fort Guijarros Museum Foundation, San Diego.

McLeod, Dean L.
2007   *Port Chicago*. Images of America Series. Arcadia Press, Charleston, SC.

McLeod, Kathy
2009   Salt and Power. Redondo Beach Historical Society, http://www.redondobeachhistorical.org/saltworks.htm, accessed December 2012.

Mealey, Marla
2009   California State Parks Archaeology at Torrey Pines State Reserve: Past Present and Future. *Proceedings of the Society of California Archaeology* 22:1–15.

Miller, Morris
1852   Letter report from Asst. Quartermaster to Major O. Cross, Chief Quartermaster, Pacific Division, US Army, San Francisco, and additional correspondence and records. 32nd Congress, 1st Session, Senate Executive Document No. 1, pp. 102–121.

Monroe, Robert D.
1959   William Birch McMurtrie: A Painter Partially Restored. *Oregon Historical Quarterly* 60(3):352–374.

Moratto, Michael J.
1984   *California Archaeology*. Academic Press, New York.

Munro-Fraser, J. P.
1880   *History of Marin County, California: Including Its Geography, Geology, Topography, and Climatography*. Alley, Bowen and Co., San Francisco.

National Park Service
2006   *Draft Channel Islands National Marine Sanctuary Management Plan*, Vol. 2. Channel Islands National Park, Ventura, CA.
2012   Presidio of San Francisco: Mexican Period, http://www.nps.gov/prsf/historyculture/mexican-period.htm, accessed October 2012.

Nelson, Nels
1907   San Francisco Bay Mounds. University of California Archaeological Survey Manuscripts No. 349. Phoebe A. Hearst Museum of Anthropology, University of California, Berkeley.
1909   Shellmounds of the San Francisco Bay Region. *University of California Publications in American Archaeology and Ethnology* 7:309–356. Berkeley.

NOAA (National Oceanic and Atmospheric Administration)
2011a   Coast and Geodetic Survey Heritage, http://www.lib.noaa.gov/noaainfo/heritage/coastandgeodeticsurvey/index.html, accessed October 2011.
2011b   Giants of Science at the US Coast Survey, http://www.history.noaa.gov/giants_index.html, accessed October 2011.
2011c   NOAA Photo Library, http://www.photolib.noaa.gov/htmls/cgs05103.htm, accessed October 2011.

NOAA (National Oceanic and Atmospheric Administration) (continued)
2012   The Coast Survey in the Civil War, 1861–1865, http://www.lib.noaa.gov/noaainfo/heritage/coastsurveyvol1/CW1.html, accessed February 2012.

Oakland Tribune
1911   Spend Vacation Digging Mounds. January 2:4.

O'Donoghue, Tom O., and Keith Punch
2003   *Qualitative Educational Research in Action: Doing and Reflecting.* Routledge Falmer, New York.

Perroy, Ryan L., Bodo Bookhagen, Oliver A. Chadwick, and Jeffrey T. Howarth
2012   Holocene and Anthropocene Landscape Change: Arroyo Formation on Santa Cruz Island, California. *Annals of the Association of American Geographers*, Vol. 6:1229–1251. Available online at http://www.geog.ucsb.edu/~bodo/pdf/perroy12_SCI_erosion.pdf.

Perry, Frank A., Robert W. Piwarzyk, Michael Luther, Alverda Orlando, Allan Molho, and Sierra L. Perry
2007   *Lime Kiln Legacies: The History of the Lime Industry in Santa Cruz County, California.* Santa Cruz Museum of Art and History, Santa Cruz.

Pettley, John W.
1998   The Mt. Diablo Initial Point, Its History and Use. *Mt. Diablo Review,* Spring 1998, Mount Diablo Surveyors Historical Society, http://www.mdshs.org/article.html, accessed November 2012.

Port Chicago Naval Magazine National Memorial
2011   Port Chicago Naval Magazine National Memorial, http://www.nps.gov/poch/index.htm, accessed December 2011.

Praetzellis, Adrian, Julia Costello, Anita Waghorn, and Eric Blind
2008   An Archaeological Research Design for El Presidio and the Main Post. The Presidio Trust, Golden Gate National Recreation Area Park Archives and Records Center, San Francisco.

Preston, Edmund B.
1890   Los Angeles County. In *California State Mining Bureau Tenth Annual Report of the State Mineralogist for the Year Ending December, 1890*, edited by W. M. Irelan, pp. 277–283. State Office, J. D. Young Supt. State Printing, Sacramento, CA.

Ransom, Leander
1873   Shell Mounds. *Proceedings of the California Academy of Sciences*, Series 1, Vol. 4, 1868–1872:86–87. San Francisco.

Rice, Arwin
2009   Port Property Picked for Planned Chetco Indian Memorial. *Curry Coastal Pilot*, November 28. Brookings-Harbor, OR.

Rick, Torben
2011 Historic Period Occupation of Anayapax, Anacapa Island, Alta California. *California Archaeology* 3(2):273–284.

Rockwell, Cleveland
1873 Topographical Map of the Site of the University of California, Berkeley, traced in 1882, 1:2,000 scale. Cartographic Records, RG 23, National Archives and Records Administration II, College Park, MD.
1878 Descriptions of Stations, Columbia River, from Kalama Upwards to Willow Bar (duplicate). GA Series R-GO-4, RG 23, National Archives and Records Administration II, College Park, MD.

Rodgers, Augustus F.
1869 Descriptions of Stations, Trinidad Head to Cape Mendocino. GA Series 13076, RG 23, National Archives and Records Administration II, College Park, MD.
1872 Descriptions of Stations, Coast North of San Francisco Bay. GA Series 13083, RG 23, National Archives and Records Administration II, College Park, MD.
1873 Wrecks to March 18, 1873, Point Pinos to Bodega Head, California. Digital file CGS05300, NOAA Central Library, Silver Spring, MD.
1887a San Diego T-sheet no. 606 (1859) with handwritten positions. GA Series 37549, RG 23, National Archives and Records Administration II, College Park, MD.
1887b Descriptions of Stations, San Diego Northward. GA Series 35805, RG 23, National Archives and Records Administration II, College Park, MD.
1894–1896 Descriptions of Stations, San Francisco Bay Resurvey. GA Series 44988, RG 23, National Archives and Records Administration II, College Park, MD.

Ruhge, Justin M.
2001 *Maritime Tragedies on the Santa Barbara Channel: A History of Shipwrecks in Fog and Storms from Point Sal to Point Mugu*. Quantum Imaging Associates, Goleta, CA.

San Francisco Call
1892 Antiquarian Researches: The *Call*'s Enterprise Commended by an Evening Contemporary. September 14:8. San Francisco.
1894 The Mounds of Alameda. October 17:6. San Francisco.
1911 Students Digging in Bay Shore Shell Mound. January 3. San Francisco.

San Francisco Estuary Institute
2012 US Coast Survey Maps of California, http://www.caltsheets.org/, accessed July 2012.

San Jose Public Library
2011 Photo csj_ARB-A005 (unknown photographer). King Library Digital Collections, http://digitalcollections.sjlibrary.org/cdm/singleitem/collection/arbuckle/id/279/rec/1283, accessed November 2012.

San Luis Obispo Tribune
1878 November 23:1, col. 5.

San Mateo Times and Daily News Leader
1929 Approaches to Bridge Built by Dutton Co. March 1:6-B, col. 5–6.

Saxe, W. E.
1875 Observations on a Shellmound at Laguna Creek, 6 miles north of Santa Cruz. *Proceedings of the California Academy of Sciences*, Series 1, Vol. 5, 1873–1874:157. San Francisco.

Schneider, Tsim D.
2007 The Role of Archived Photographs in Native California Archaeology. *Journal of Social Archaeology* 7(1):49–71.

Schumacher, Paul
1874 Ancient Graves and Shell Heaps of California. *Smithsonian Institution Annual Report for 1874*:335–350. Smithsonian Institution, Washington, DC.
1877 Aboriginal Settlements of the Pacific Coast. *Popular Science Monthly* 10(57):353–356.

Schwartz, Steve
2010 The Lost Indian Cave of San Nicolas Island. Manuscript on file, Naval Air Warfare Center, Camarillo, CA.
2012a Archaeological Site Record for San Nicolas Island Site AB-22. Manuscript on file, Naval Air Warfare Center, Camarillo, CA.
2012b The Search for the Lost Indian Cave of San Nicolas Island. Paper presented at the 8th California Islands Symposium, Catalina Islands Conservancy, Ventura, CA.

Schwemmer, Robert V.
2008 The Mystery Shipwreck: Uncovering Oregon's Historic Past. *Oregon Coast Magazine* June/July:46–49.

Scofield, William L.
1954 *California Fishing Ports*. California Fish and Game Bulletin 96. Available online at http://www.escholarship.org/uc/item/5b62j14p.

Sengteller, Louis A.
1870 Description of Stations, Punta Arena Vicinity (duplicate). GA Series 13077, RG 23, National Archives and Records Administration II, College Park, MD.
1871 Description of Stations, San Luis Obispo Bay, California (duplicate). GA Series 2662, RG 23, National Archives and Records Administration II, College Park, MD.
1871–1873 Description of Stations, Navarro River to Noyo River, Mendocino County (duplicate). GA Series, RG 23, National Archives and Records Administration II, College Park, MD.
1876–1879 Descriptions of Stations, Fort Ross to Point Arena (duplicate). GA Series 31992½, RG 23, National Archives and Records Administration II, College Park, MD.

Shalowitz, Aaron L.
1964 *Shore and Sea Boundaries with Special Reference to the Interpretation and the Use of Coast and Geodetic Survey Data*, Vol. 2. US Department of Commerce Publication 10-1. US Government Printing Office, Washington, DC.

Slotten, Hugh Richard
1994   *Patronage, Practice, and the Culture of American Science: Alexander Dallas Bache and the US Coast Survey*. Cambridge University Press, New York.

Soule, Frank
1855   The Mission and Presidio of San Francisco. In *Annals of San Francisco*, pp. 162–172. D. Appleton and Co., New York.

Squier, Ephraim, and Edwin Davis
1848   Ancient Monuments of the Mississippi Valley. *Smithsonian Contributions to Knowledge*, Vol. 1. Smithsonian Institution, Washington, DC.

Stearns, Robert E. C.
1873   Aboriginal Shell Money. *Proceedings of the California Academy of Sciences*, Series 1, Vol. 4, 1868–1872:118–120. San Francisco.

Stenzel, Franz
1972   *Cleveland Rockwell, Scientist and Artist, 1837–1907*. Oregon Historical Society, Portland, OR.
1975   *James Madison Alden: Yankee Artist of the Pacific Coast, 1854–1860*. Amon Carter Museum, Fort Worth, TX.

Stewart, Suzanne, and Adrian Praetzellis
2003   Archaeological Research Issues for the Point Reyes National Seashore–Golden Gate National Recreation Area. Archaeological Studies Center, Sonoma State University, Rohnert Park, CA.

Taylor, Alexander
1860   The Indianology of California No. 9. *California Farmer and Journal of Useful Sciences* 12(12):90, May 11.

Thalman, Sylvia B.
1993   *The Coast Miwok Indians of the Point Reyes Area*. Point Reyes National Seashore Association, Point Reyes, CA.

Theberge, Captain Albert E.
2006   Coast Surveyors on the Pioneer Coast. *Mains'l Haul*, Vol. 42(2/3):8–17. Maritime Museum of San Diego, California.
2011   *The Coast Survey 1807–1867*. History of the Commissioned Corps of the National Oceanic and Atmospheric Administration, Vol. 1. Available online at http://www.lib.noaa.gov/noaainfo/heritage/coastsurveyvol1/TITLE.html#TITLE.

Thomas Jefferson Foundation
2005   Thomas Mann Randolph, http://explorer.monticello.org/index.html?s1=0|s4=7_4, accessed March 2012.

Trent, Heidi, and Joey Seymour
2010   Examining California's First Palm Tree: The Serra Palm. *Journal of San Diego History* 56(3):105–120.

Tripcevich, Nicholas, and Scott Byram
2013   Assembling 19th-Century Coast Survey Data in GIS for Archaeological Site Identification. Paper presented at the 47th Annual Meeting of the Society for California Archaeology, Berkeley, CA.

Tveskov, Mark A., and Amie Cohen
2008   *The Fort Lane Archaeology Project*. Southern Oregon University Laboratory of Anthropology Research Report 2007-1, Ashland, OR.

United States Coast and Geodetic Survey
1857   Sub-sketch of Point Hueneme, http://www.photolib.noaa.gov/htmls/cgs05171.htm, accessed December 2012.
1871–1875 Descriptions of Stations, Magdalena Bay 1871–75. GA Series 13089, RG 23, National Archives and Records Administration II, College Park, MD.
1891   Hydrographic Chart 5909, Chetko Cove (1870 topography).

United States Court of Claims
1931   Coos (or Kowes) Bay, Lower Umpqua (or Kalowatset), and Siuslaw Indian Tribes vs. the United States of America. Testimony Taken on Behalf of Claimants, November 10th to 13th, 1931. Document on file, Coquille Indian Tribe, North Bend, OR.

United States Surveyor-General of California
1876   *Before the United States Surveyor-General of California, in the Matter of the Rancho Corte Madero del Presidio*. Francis, Valentine, and Co., San Francisco.

University of Alabama
2011   Historical Map Collection Online, US Coast Survey, http://alabamamaps.ua.edu/historicalmaps/Coastal%20Survey%20Maps/, accessed December 2012.

Vellanoweth, René, Patricia Martz, and Steven Schwartz
2002   The Late Holocene Archaeology of San Nicolas Island. In *Catalysts to Complexity: Late Holocene Societies of the California Coast*, edited by Jon Erlandson and Terry Jones, pp. 82–100. Cotsen Institute, University of California, Los Angeles.

Wagner, Henry R.
1932   George Davidson, Geographer of the Northwest Coast of America. *California Historical Society Quarterly* 11:299–320.

Wallenburg, Charles
2002   *Berkeley: A City in History*. University of California Press, Berkeley.

Ward, Beverly
1986   *White Moccasins*. Myrtle Point Printing, Myrtle Point, OR.

Wells, William
1856   Wild Life in Oregon. *Harper's New Monthly Magazine* 47:98–99.

Wolfram, Andrew
2010   *Presidio Officers Club Building 50 Historic Structure Report*. The Presidio Trust, Golden Gate National Recreation Area Park Archives and Records Center, San Francisco.

Woodbury, Nathalie F.
1960   Notes and News. *American Antiquity* 26(2):310.

Yu, Ellen
1995   Geodetic Investigation of the Hayward Earthquake of 1868. Unpublished Master's thesis, Department of Geophysics, Stanford University, Stanford, CA.

Zwinger, Ann H. (editor)
1987   *Xantus: The Letters of John Xantus to Spencer Fullerton Baird from San Francisco and Cabo San Lucas 1859–1861*. Dawson's Book Shop, Los Angeles.